SWEET LAND

of

LIBERTY

An American's Account
of His Experiences
as a Japanese POW

TALMADGE A. SMITHEY

ISBN 978-1-64669-868-4

*This book is dedicated to Talmadge A. Smithey and those who served
with him in maintaining the freedom and liberty we all enjoy today.*

I'd like to acknowledge the efforts of my friend Tim Porter, who helped bring these accounts from my uncle to life. And, also the efforts of Tom Symalla, who transcribed the stories and edited the book.

— **Scotty L. Smithey**

Table of Contents

Foreword

Talmadge Smithey was my uncle. When I was a young man, I remember hearing stories that my uncle was a war hero. He had been captured by the Japanese in World War II and had endured years of hardship as a Japanese prisoner of war.

As a young man, I always found my uncle's stories to be fascinating, even though he never talked a lot about his experiences as a POW. I never understood the full scope of the sacrifices he made and the hardships he endured until after he passed away in 1999.

After he passed, among the things he left behind were his notes from his experiences as a POW. As my family and I read this account of his experiences, we realized the significance of the sacrifices of my uncle and the fellow Americans who endured the same or similar hardships in an effort to maintain and secure the freedom and liberty which we as Americans are now accustomed to.

As you read my uncle's account of his experiences as a Japanese prisoner of war, I'm sure you'll agree that, like many of the men who have fought for our freedom before and since World War II, he had a story to tell.

What follows is my uncle's account of his experiences. Hopefully, his story will remind us all of the sacrifices that have been made for the freedom we enjoy as Americans, freedom we sometimes take for granted.

Scotty L. Smithey

The Day Everything Changed

It was just another day in the Philippines when we got the news. Our ship, the *USS Canopus,* was anchored in Manila Bay. It was December 8, 1941. I was the ship's carpenter. As usual, I was ashore with the Liberty Section of our crew, when we received the urgent message to report back to the ship immediately. My shipmates and I were curious about what could prompt such a request.

Back aboard the ship, in an assembly, we were all informed that the Japanese had attacked Pearl Harbor the day before. We wondered what that meant, but many of us knew immediately that the Japanese attack of US ships in Pearl Harbor was an act of war. We were instructed to act accordingly and to take immediate measures to prepare the ship for war. We didn't know it then, but that was the day everything changed, for us and for many Americans. The world was at war and we were smack-dab in the middle of it.

Immediately, we applied blue paint to the grey exterior of the ship, the idea being that the blue paint would help disguise our ship and make it less identifiable against the blue of the ocean for Japanese bomber planes. We removed all necessary materials from the ship and landed it at Cavite. Service ammunition was placed in the ready boxes as we worked earnestly to prepare the *Canopus* for war.

At 9 a.m. that day, the first air raid siren sounded on the ship. We waited for hours for something to happen, but nothing happened, at least not in our vicinity. My shipmates and I were relieved.

Hours later, at 8 p.m., the air raid sirens sounded again. This time we could see the Japanese planes flying overhead as they headed toward Nicholas Field, the airfield that housed our fleet of airplanes. It wasn't long after those Japanese planes had flown over us that we could see the rosy glow of fuel dumps burning, lighting the horizon. No good could come from that, I thought, when I saw the lit area in the distance. My suspicions were later confirmed when we found out that most of the fighter planes intended to defend the Philippines had been destroyed or disabled by the Japanese attack.

With news of this raid, the *Canopus* pulled up anchor, moved a short distance and docked at Pier 1 in Manila. Immediately, the crew spread fishnets over the *Canopus*, and painted red the weather decks and superstructures of the ship, hoping that the red paint would allow the ship to blend in with the red roofs of the nearby warehouses. We hoped that the ship would not be an easy target for Japanese bomber planes.

At the same time we painted the ship in the hopes it wouldn't be hit, we prepared for it to be hit. We removed most of the supplies, provisions, and fuel oil from the ship and preparations were made to scuttle the ship alongside the cock to keep it from capsizing if hit by a Japanese bomb.

Soon after, we counted 54 Japanese planes as they flew over in V formation, much like a flock of geese. The planes made two practice runs before releasing their bombs on the third run, and then flying a reconnaissance over Corregidor before presumably returning to the Japanese air base in Formosa. Fortunately, we had been spared. We told ourselves that we would live to see at least another day.

During the Japanese air raid, all US ships fired upon them, but without any success. We already knew the reason for the lack of success. Ammunition fired from the three-inch guns of the ships could reach a maximum altitude of 17,000 feet. The Japanese were well aware of this, so they flew their planes at altitudes of 18,000 and 19,000 feet.

"Where were the US fighter planes?", you ask. Well, most of the US fighter planes were still on the drawing board, in the planning stages. The US was not ready for the war, at least not in the Philippines. Americans honored treaties that had been previously signed, and we expected other countries to do likewise. The Japanese attacks on US ships and planes were totally unexpected and left the US somewhat unprepared, at least in the Philippines.

Outnumbered and Outgunned

After the air raids near Manila Bay, we had to rely on newspaper and radio accounts regarding what was happening. Those accounts gave us the news that the Japanese had landed 80 transports at Lingayen Gulf. And five other Japanese landings were made simultaneously on Luzon. The Japanese were serious in their attempt to secure the Philippines.

A local radio commentator summed up the situation by telling listeners, "Eighty Japanese transports have landed troops at the Lingayen Gulf and the USAFFE (United States Air Force Far East) has contacted them, and, if you will pardon my saying, is giving them hell. The little brown men from Nippon can't fight with their glasses on and they certainly can't fight with them off—Keep 'em flying!"

We learned later that this radio account had been inaccurate, as most of the Japanese landings had been without opposition, and the American army had withdrawn to Bataan Peninsula, where they planned to make a stand against Japanese forces that outnumbered them and against military equipment which left them with little chance for victory.

All of the US ships and submarines were prepped to depart the Philippines and sail for Australia. Crews worked diligently and with purpose to prepare the likes of the *Canopus, Sea Lion, Sea Dragon, Quail, Tangier, Pigeon, Finch, Vega, Ranger,* and *Genesee* to sail for Australia. Most of the vessels were small tugs and minesweepers, except for the *Canopus, Sea Lion,* and *Sea Dragon.* The *Sea Lion* never made it out of harbor, as it was found to be in disrepair and not fit for sea. Instead, it was demolished.

The crew of the *Canopus* worked on the *Sea Dragon* day and night for five days, making her fit for the trip to Australia, where she later played an important role in the war.

The *Canopus,* on the other hand, quickly loaded her supplies, provisions, and fuel oil, leaving Manila for Mariveles Bay on Christmas Eve, December 24. I remember the huge fires glowing from Manila as we left Manila Bay. Filipinos were looting the city as US demolition squads were blowing up and destroying fuel and ammunition dumps before leaving Manila to its unfortunate fate. In destroying the fuel and ammunition dumps, the US was assured that they would not be leaving these resources to the Japanese as they came through the city.

We anchored in Mariveles Bay, where we tied up in a cove shortly after daybreak on Christmas Day. Christmas was far from our minds as we cut branches and boughs from the nearby jungle areas and hauled them to the ship to use as camouflage. We placed branches on the decks of the ship and tied boughs to the mast in hopes of hiding the ship from the Japanese. Once again, we used paint to try to disguise our ship so the Japanese would not discover it. This time we used green paint to cover the red paint that had previously been used on the exterior of the ship.

We learned quickly that our efforts were useless. Japanese bombers found the ship and bombed her, killing seven crew members and injuring several others.

Our anti-aircraft gunners had stayed at their stations, but their attacks on the Japanese planes were largely ineffective.

The US submarine *Trout* brought 21 fuses for the anti-aircraft at Corregidor. When news leaked out about the staggering US losses at Pearl Harbor, the *Trout* took $20 million worth of gold from Corregidor, for safekeeping from the Japanese.

The Japanese army swept south, successfully taking Hong Kong, Java, Sumatra, The Celebes, and part of New Guinea. However, Bataan and Corregidor remained strong against Japanese opposition.

General MacArthur spoke to the US and Filipino troops. "Bataan and Corregidor cannot and will not be surrendered. We must fight; if you retreat, you will lose your life. Help is coming; hundreds of planes and thousands of men are coming, but they have to fight their way through thousands of miles of enemy-infested waters."

Soon after, with the fall of Singapore to the Japanese, more Japanese forces were sent to the Philippines and the fighting there intensified. Air raids that had already been frequent became even more frequent.

Surrender

The crew of the *Canopus* was sent ashore daily at 7 a.m. We had burned oil barrels filled with rags in the hopes of giving the Japanese the impression that the *Canopus* was a burned-out hulk. This plan seemed to deceive the Japanese reconnaissance photographers, as the Japanese didn't bother the ship anymore.

In March, 1942, General MacArthur, his wife, son, and some of his staff, left in PT (Patrol Torpedo) boats for Del Norte in Mindanao, one of the largest islands in the Philippines. The PT boats transported MacArthur and company safely to Mindanao, from where they were flown to Australia.

Soon after, the Japanese implored the Filipinos to surrender, dropping pamphlets from airplanes and broadcasting on Japanese radio that "MacArthur has left the Philippines and there is no one left to protect you now."

Some of the pamphlets gave instructions on how to surrender. Others showed photos of beautiful girls offering a kiss. Radio programs from Manila addressed Americans at Bataan: "And to you Americans at Bataan, the world's largest self-supporting concentration camp, why do you continue to fight? You are sick, hungry, and longing for your loved ones.

For you Americans, we dedicate this song." The songs that followed included *"They're Waiting for the Ships that Never Came In"*, *"Old Folks at Home"*, *"Old Black Joe"*, and *"My Old Kentucky Home"*. All songs selected were picked with the objective in mind to encourage American soldiers to feel homesick and to give up the fight.

As days passed, hunger malaria, dysentery, and war casualties all took their toll. The defenders of Bataan were battling Japanese forces that appeared to be growing. Our PT boats were now gone, our submarines no longer came to be repaired, and we no longer spotted any of our B-17 planes. Hope was waning. Where was the convoy that was supposedly on its way?

On April 17, the crew of the *Canopus* worked all night to remove all valuable items from the ship. We removed bedding, clothing, provisions, food, and other useful articles. The *Canopus* was then scuttled in broad daylight to prevent capture of the ship by the Japanese. For many of us, scuttling the *Canopus* was akin to abandoning an old friend, but we all understood that it was necessary.

The officers and crew of the scuttled ship were then taken to Corregidor, where the crew and junior officers were placed in the Marine beach defense.

The next day, April 18, at 8 a.m., Bataan surrendered to the Japanese. Americans captured at Bataan were prepared to make the 81-mile march to Camp O'Donnell in the Tarlac Province. This march later become known as the "Bataan Death March" or the "Death March to O'Donnell".

In unrelenting heat, we were led toward Camp O'Donnell without food or water. Many prisoners succumbed to the heat. As the march continued, we were losing fellow soldiers at the rate of 100-200 a day. Those of us who survived would learn later that up to 20,000 Americans and Filipinos had died in that march. Even those that were surviving were weakened so much that death seemed imminent.

For about a week after the surrender, some of the captives sent out SOS (Save Our Ship/Save Our Souls) flashes at night from the beaches of Bataan. Still, no help came. Eventually, the captives wondered whether it would ever come. Eventually, the captives came to view the SOS flashes as useless and pathetic, and those efforts were discontinued.

Some of the captives managed to secure small boats or rafts in the four or five days following the surrender. They used these small vessels to reach Corregidor. Men arriving at Corregidor sent back word that things there were bleak for Americans, as the Japanese there were killing all Americans.

By this time, the small isle of Corregidor was in absolute shambles. All of the buildings had been reduced to rubble by artillery fire. Trees and shrubs had been splintered; craters from bombs and artillery shells pockmarked the entire island. Gun batteries located in nearby Batangas Province had shelled the isle since February, 1943, and, with the fall of Bataan, the Japanese moved hundreds of siege guns to the front and shelled the fortress, as well as Fort Hughes, which had been built by the US Army in the early 1900s to protect Manila and Subic Bay. Japanese bombers leaving from Clark Field unleashed an estimated 200,000 rounds of artillery shells in demolishing the forts during the last 10 days of the siege. The anti-aircraft batteries that had previously protected the fort had been knocked out, and the Japanese were able to attack the forts without much opposition.

In Corregidor, our food was being rationed. We were given two meals a day, those meals consisting mostly of cracked wheat, wieners, and coffee. The continuous shelling and bombing prohibited us from cooking. Many of us were getting weak from the insufficient rations.

The arrival of May brought even more shelling and bombing. Submarines had been coming into Corregidor and taking out some men. The captain of the *Canopus*, some radiomen, the repair officers, and some metalsmiths were evacuated from Corregidor by submarine. At the same time, PBYs landed in the bay at night and retrieved additional personnel, including seven nurses. PBYs were amphibious aircraft that were often used for patrol bombing, convoy escort, search and rescue missions, cargo transport, and anti-submarine warfare. Obviously, the submarines and the PBYs were able to rescue only a selected few. For those of us left behind, the situation became more and more hopeless.

On May 5 at sunset, the Japanese began firing on Corregidor with a heavy barrage of artillery. Thousands of artillery shells mewed and exploded. Japanese landing barges appeared out of the darkness. Our machine gunners and infantrymen met the Japanese and the battle raged all night into the afternoon of May 6.

Casualties were heavy on both sides. When dawn arrived, Japanese planes appeared, and Japanese tanks, flame throwers, and field pieces were landed in an onslaught that would produce devastation for American and Filipino troops. Many of the wounded Americans and Filipinos were taken to the back of the line. With Japanese flame throwers on the way, we received orders to withdraw and fight. Without any artillery left to knock out the flame throwers, we knew that our fighting would only delay the inevitable.

Finally, the US flag was hauled down and replaced by a white flag of surrender. Despite the white flag, the shelling and strife continued for a while.

What Happens Now?

When the fighting finally stopped, order broke down. Men started wandering around aimlessly, wondering what to do now. Some men looked for their buddies; some fellow Navy men were desperately trying to locate their shipmates.

In the Queen and Malinta Tunnels, important papers and documents were burned and paper money was destroyed in an effort to prevent it from getting into the hands of the Japanese. Food which had previously been hoarded was now readily available and free to anyone who wanted it, despite the protests of the quartermaster who had previously issued it.

Thousands of Americans and Filipinos lined the tunnels, none of them sure what would happen now that the US had surrendered. Men returning from the front lines began eating the food and drinking the water. Most men were smoking.

Orders were received to discard all guns, hand grenades, bayonets, and ammunition.

The first Japanese to arrive at the tunnels were the tank operators. Upon arrival, the first thing they did was to rush to the tunnels for water. The water system had been knocked out, but the Japanese restored it and water became available quickly…for the Japanese.

I remember well the Japanese officer who came through the tunnel holding an American .45 automatic in both hands. He said nothing, but seemed surprised at the number of Americans and Filipinos who had survived the siege. I also remember well how dense the tunnel was with cigarette smoke, from men who chain-smoked as they pondered their pending fate.

In the night that followed the final battle, more Japanese soldiers came to the island. And many of them came through the tunnels, looking for valuables from the American and Filipino soldiers—items such as watches, fountain pens, rings, money, gold-rimmed eyeglasses, and sweet foods such as jellies, jams, honey, preserves, sugar, and pineapples. Most of the Japanese soldiers could not read English, and if a can had an attractive label, they would thrust a bayonet into it. If the can contained meat, vegetables, or unsweetened food, the Japanese seemed to have no interest in it and would discard it. But if the can contained sweets, the Japanese kept it, considering it a valued commodity.

Pineapples in particular became a favorite of the Japanese, so much so that many Japanese soldiers quickly learned the English word for pineapple and were frequently asking us if we had any pineapple.

Outside the tunnels, more Japanese occupation forces continued to arrive. Americans were pressed into service to bring the bags of the Japanese ashore. Looting was widespread. I witnessed a scene in which a Japanese officer asked for some American officers to guide him on an inspection tour. Two American officers volunteered for the duty. The Japanese officer accompanied them for just a short while until they had reached a more isolated area and then pointed a gun at the two American officers before promptly relieving them of their money, watches, and rings. The Japanese officer than apologized to the Americans before letting them go, but keeping the valuables he had confiscated.

On May 9, three days after the battle had ended, we received orders to prepare to leave on a five-day march and to take some food with us. The Japanese split us into groups of 100 and told us to march four abreast out of the tunnels, around the winding road in an area known as Ninety-Second Garage on the south shore of Corregidor. Each incoming column of prisoners was counted and recounted by the Japanese guards before being dismissed into the area which was in shambles due to the recent bombing and shelling.

Some prisoners had been assembled and retained in this area since the surrender. Again, water was at a premium. I heard stories that the prisoners there had even drained the radiators of the tractors and trucks there, desperate for water to drink. An emergency seepage spring had been dug near the seaplane hangar. A bucket tied on a line was in continuous operation to keep the thousands of thirsty men from perishing, but the spring would be dipped dry and we'd then have to wait for more water to seep back in.

After repeated requests, the Japanese finally allowed prisoners to form columns of 100 and took them to the Malinta Tunnel for water. A tunnel complex built by the US Army Corps of Engineers, the Malinta Tunnel had been used as a bomb-proof storage and personnel bunker. In the tunnel, water was now flowing through a trough that had been previously used as a toilet. Occasionally, a Japanese soldier would have an American prisoner wash a pair of trousers or a shirt in the water. Regardless of the circumstances, we were so desperate for water, we didn't care about its history. We waited patiently in line for our turn at the trough.

The Japanese drafted prisoners to work to perform daily tasks and other tasks. We heard horrid stories from the prisoners who were charged with burying the dead. Japanese instructed the prisoners to lop off the right hand of every dead Japanese soldier. The disbelieving American soldiers on this death detail wondered why the Japanese had instructed them to cut off these hands at the wrist. After the hands had been removed from the bodies of the dead Japanese, the bodies were then stacked up and burned. We later learned that the Japanese separately burned the right hands of the dead soldiers and the ashes from the individual hands were then placed in urns and returned to Japan for burial in their shrines.

What happened with the dead Americans? While American prisoners were tending to the dead Japanese, dead Americans remained where they had fallen for four or five days. You can probably imagine the condition of the dead bodies after laying for days in the tropical heat.

Finally, we were able to convince the Japanese to allow us to bury the bodies. That being said, not a single American body received a proper burial. Bombshell craters were often used as the graves and there was seldom enough dirt to cover the bodies we placed in the craters. Some soldiers tried to say prayers over the new graves, but were often interrupted by the Japanese and told to move along to bury the next body. The American soldiers who returned from these death details would never forget those experiences.

When the bomb craters were not being used as shallow graves, these craters and revetments and ditches were used as latrines. Flies were extremely thick in the areas of the latrines.

As a result, using the latrines wasn't something any of us looked forward to.

The Japanese didn't make any arrangements to feed us. We were on our own. All prisoners were left to fend and forage for themselves. Some prisoner groups were able to steal food from the Japanese as they served on various chore details, but at the risk of severe beatings and even execution if caught. Prisoners got together and pooled their food, but there was never enough.

Just as there was no food, there was also no shelter for the prisoners. The airplane hangars had been riddled by shrapnel and gunfire. Every group of prisoners jerry-rigged sheets, blankets, and coats to produce much desired shade from the hot sun.

Dysentery was prevalent now. Water was very scarce. The only bathing area available was the sea, which was often misused and contaminated. Some soldiers, desperate for water to drink, drank some of the sea water and soon fell sick. Some of those soldiers even died from drinking the contaminated sea water.

Working parties of prisoners started removing food from the tunnels and placing it in small ship at the dock. Eventually, several tons of goods had been stacked near the compound. Other prisoner parties began collecting guns and ammunition, while other parties collected non-ferrous metal and scrap iron.

There were some instances of Japanese guards mistreating the prisoners, slapping them or hitting them with rifles, but for the most part, the treatment was fair—especially when compared to the treatment we would later receive.

Rumors ran rampant among prisoners in the camp. One rumor was that five American transports were on the way from Australia to take us home. With the Germans at Stalingrad, England fighting for its life, and the Japanese moving unchecked toward Australia, the future looked bad for us. Beyond the Pacific, America was forging arms and armor; men were being marshaled to fight. We had no doubt that America would win the war. But we didn't know how and we also knew that America was a long way from where we were imprisoned by the Japanese.

Seventeen dreary days passed at Ninety-Second Garage. We fought the hot sun, hunger, thirst, and flies during the days; we fought mosquitoes at night, longing for places to sleep comfortably.

***

On the night of May 23, heavy rains came. Everyone and everything got wet. Around 9 p.m., word was passed that we should prepare to leave at 6 a.m. the following day. Long before daylight, preparations were being made to leave. Most of us rolled our essential possessions into a blanket or towel. Only the items that could be carried by hand were packed. The other larger and heavier items would have to be left behind.

Some men had been able to hide and retain valuables such as money, watches, rings, and pens. Some of these valuables had been hidden under bandages with the idea that the Japanese would never check there, as medical care was almost non-existent. Men who had valuables hidden on their person had found that the best way to avoid a body search by the Japanese was to start coughing and scratching just before the Japanese were getting ready to initiate a search. We found that most of the Japanese were afraid of germs and the possibility of disease. A Japanese soldier conducting inspections, upon seeing a coughing and scratching American prisoner, would almost always move on to the next soldier without inspecting the sickly soldiers.

The Trip to Manila

By 7 a.m. that day of May 23, all of the prisoners had been formed into columns and we started marching slowly toward the dock area. Once there, we were herded into a gravel pit, where we waited under the unbearable sun while small fishing boats transported us to one of two rusty freighters in the bay.

Aboard the fishing boats, the Japanese soldiers were again inspecting our possessions and asking us for money. One of the Japanese soldiers had confiscated one of the prisoners' tobacco pouch, mostly, we think, because it had a fancy zipper. The Japanese soldier was surprised and delighted when he found 500 pesos ($250) nestled in the tobacco.

In placing us on the ships, the Japanese separated the American prisoners from the Filipino prisoners. We later learned that there were about 7600 American prisoners in this group. Hospital staff, nurses, doctors, and the severely wounded were left behind to be transported later. We later found out that the nurses were taken to the University of Santo Thomas, where they were repatriated (sent back to their home country) on January 1, 1943. We heard that the nurses were treated respectfully by the Japanese; to my knowledge, none of them was assaulted or molested.

The Fourth Marine's mascot, Suchow, was aboard the ship with us as we were transported to Manila. Suchow was a remarkable dog who survived three years of internment at Cabanatuan. In a time of ultimate despair, Suchow was a beacon of hope to American prisoners; he never lacked for attention or food.

Later, when Rangers finally rescued the prisoners at Cabanatuan, those prisoners and Suchow were taken to Leyte. The men were returned to America aboard a ship, but Suchow was denied passage. One of the Fourth Marines was left behind in the Philippines to take care of Suchow. Both of them were then flown to the States, arriving before the ship full of former American prisoners arrived. When Suchow later died, he was given an honorable burial by the Marines, who had realized the value of his "service".

Conditions were crowded beyond imagination on the ship headed to Manila. It was impossible to move about. Sanitary measures were extremely crude. Although there was sufficient water to drink, there was no food to eat.

We spent the night on the anchored ship, which hadn't yet moved. At dawn on May 25, the old ship picked up anchor and sailed toward Manila. Upon anchoring in Manila, we were quickly herded on to landing barges. These barges would take a load of men within 200 to 300 yards of the shore before the men were instructed to jump into about four feet of water and go to shore. Men who were reluctant to jump into the water were given assistance with that, hit on the head with a boat hook at the hands of a Japanese soldier. In this process, some prisoners lost their shoes; others abandoned their baggage after it became wet and heavy.

When all of us had arrived ashore, the Japanese cavalry again assembled us in columns of 100 and marched us to Dewey Boulevard. About 10 a.m. that day, what became known as the "March of Shame" or the "Dewey Boulevard Parade" began. Flanked by Japanese soldiers, we were forced to march over six miles down Dewey Boulevard toward the Bilibid Prison. With this march down Dewey Boulevard, the Japanese wanted to show the Filipino people who lined the streets that they had conquered the Americans and that they were the superior race; white men and black men were inferior to them.

The tropical sun was too much for many of the starved Americans, who were forced to keep walking without rest. The streets became littered with men who had collapsed. The men who lost their shoes coming off the landing barges suffered severely blistered feet as the walk progressed. Japanese sentries were stationed at all intersections, building entrances, and alleys. There was no chance for escape, even for the few men who had the energy to do so.

Thousands of Filipinos lined the street to see the spectacle, the parade of prisoners. Some of them wept. Others flashed "V" signs to the Americans. Some Filipinos tried to deliver food, candies, or cigarettes to the destitute American prisoners, but their efforts were rebuffed and thwarted by the Japanese soldiers.

The march for which the Japanese had intended to humiliate American prisoners and trumpet the prestige of the Japanese, had the adverse effect on the Filipinos, who saw the starving American prisoners and empathized with them.

As the heat along the route increased, more and more of the Americans discarded their baggage. It was just too heavy to carry in the overwhelming tropical heat. Garbage cans full of water had been placed near the Admiral Hotel and the prisoners were allowed a quick drink from a tin cup as we passed the area. Unfortunately, all of the water was consumed before even half the men had passed.

Men who had been overcome with heat and collapsed along the route were often kicked by the Japanese guards as the men lay on the ground. The men who couldn't get up and continue were later collected and delivered to Bilibin Prison in trucks.

As we marched, many Filipino onlookers would whisper the number of kilometers remaining until we reached the prison. Those of us who hadn't known our destination at the beginning of the march,, knew full well where we were headed as we continued to march. The Filipinos along the way made sure of that.

By 5 p.m. that day, the last of the prisoner columns reached Bilibad, the former prison of the Philippines. With the breakdown of law and order resulting from the recent battles, all Filipino prisoners had been released, and all fixtures, including plumbing, had been removed from the prison. The high walls remained intact.

By the time all prisoners had arrived at Bilibid, the prison was terribly overcrowded. About 12,000 men filled an area that had been designed for 4000. Every inch of space was taken up. Exhausted and famished, we slept on concrete floors, as closely together as possible. For the first time since our surrender, the Japanese fed us…a small portion of rice.

Japanese guards patrolled the walls of the prison, while others circulated among the prisoners, still looking for valuables. Some of the guards on top of the wall would lower strings down to the prisoners, who would then attach money to the string in exchange for treats such as molasses, coconut, popcorn, or native candy, which was later found to be contaminated and causing dysentery

Some of the prisoners had medicine and were trying to sell it to some of the other prisoners who still had hidden money. Quinine, sulfa drugs, and aspirin were all in great demand and were worth their weight in gold.

Cabanatuan

In the following days, a large group of prisoners was evacuated each day, their fate and their destinations unknown. The prisoners would be marched to the railroad station, where 80 to 100 men would be crammed like cattle into a boxcar with a Japanese guard at each door. We learned later that the trains were taking us to the Cabanatuan prison camp in North Luzon, where we would be later joined by surviving Americans from Camp O'Donnell.

The group I left with departed Bilibid on May 29. As you can imagine, the heat inside the boxcars was unbearable. The Japanese guards would not allow the men with dysentery to get out of the cars to relieve themselves, so the stench inside the car was overwhelming.

Upon arrival at Cabanatuan, we were marched to the schoolhouse there, where we were given some rice and told to prepare for 20-kilometer (12.4 miles) hike the next day. We were told to consider our baggage and discard any items we wouldn't need.

At 3 a.m. the next day, we were awakened and given another ration of rice. We were then again assembled in columns and marched on to the road, where we were told to sit down and wait. About 8 a.m., we began another march. The sun's heat had already begun to absorb the moisture from the previous night's rain and the humidity was thick.

Enterprising Filipinos had set up stands along the road lining the route. They were selling an assortment of foods, including boiled eggs, calesa pony sugar, homemade candies, rice cakes, popped rice, bananas, sugar, peanuts, and tobacco. Unfortunately for them and unfortunately for the marching prisoners, the Japanese guards would not allow the prisoners to purchase foods from the roadside stands.

Empathetic Filipinos even tried to give us food, but were thwarted in their attempts by Japanese guards. An old grey-haired woman, weeping and mumbling something about her son, broke into our ranks and started handing out rice cakes before a Japanese guard caught up with her and beat her to the ground.

Guards were changed every two or three miles, as we continued our march. The sun was getting hotter and hotter; perspiration was raining from the men. Canteens were empty and there was no place along the way to refill them. Men began collapsing from fatigue, heat, and exhaustion. Vicious guards would soundly beat any man who collapsed, jabbing them with rifle butts and stomping them with boots. Some of the fallen men rejoined the ranks after they'd been pummeled; others could not get up. Seeing those beatings, all of us had an intense dread of fainting or collapsing. We wanted to do whatever possible to stay on our feet.

If a prisoner was unconscious or could not get up after his collapse or beating, the Japanese guards would place a tall stick with a piece of paper on the top of the stick beside the fallen prisoner. These prisoners were later collected by a truck hauling rice to our future camp.

At 5 p.m. that day, we finally reached Camp #2, a camp that had originally been built for the Philippine army. Unfortunately, construction of the camp was never completed, and, as a result, it was without water. We were all thirsty and some of the men were raving.

At sunset, a heavy rain came and, after drinking all of the rainwater we could handle, we were able to bathe in the water that fell from the straw-covered barracks. We then filled every available container with precious, precious water and were thankful that Merciful Heaven had provided for us in our time of desperation. After sunset, a small amount of rice that had been cooked at Camp #3 arrived by truck.

Camp #1, My Home for 23 Months

After spending two days at Camp #2, we were ordered to prepare to leave. We marched about four miles over the same route we'd traveled before, to Camp #1. I didn't know it then, but Camp #1 would be my home for the next 23 months.

During the month of June, the month after I arrived at Camp #1, 501 prisoners died at Cabanatuan. Malaria, dysentery, beriberi, diphtheria, and many other ailments took their toll. As a lot, my fellow prisoners and I were horrible to behold. There were no bathing facilities and there were few razors among the prisoners. Malnutrition affected individuals differently. Some individuals had agonizing pains which seemed to attack every bone and muscle in their body. Every possible remedy was tried for this malnutrition, including pacing the ground, soaking feet in water, and foot massages. Very seldomly did any of these remedies work, but we were desperate to stop the pain.

Some prisoners would swell to grotesque proportions. Faces would swell until the eyes closed. Hands swelled to the size of boxing gloves, fingers to the size of sausages, and feet resembled footballs. Usually, after stomachs began to swell, death was close behind.

On some of the starving prisoners, the rudimentary glands would swell. On some prisoners, their eyes became inflamed, constantly discharging tears when exposed to light. As a result, some of the prisoners who suffered from this malady created eye shields out of pasteboard, cutting slits or eyeholes into the pasteboard. Cod liver oil was scarce in the camp, but some of the prisoners with inflamed eyes used drops of cod liver oil in their eyes in an attempt to remedy the problem.

Late in 1942, the Japanese confiscated some Filipino drug store stocks and brought some medicines into the camp. Some of the medications included home remedies such as: *Winter Smith's Chill Tonic, Sixty-Six Chill Tonic, Wine of Cardui, Black Draught, Silver Pine Healing Oil, Simon's Liver Regulator, Syrup of Pepsin,* and many other remedies. The Japanese weren't sure what these medications were for, because most of them couldn't read English, but they distributed the medications and potions to their American prisoners nonetheless. Like the Americans, but to an obvious much lesser extent, the Japanese were also hoping to get rid of some of the illnesses and diseases which were prevalent in the camp.

The American doctors in the camp tried everything possible to save the ailing prisoners, but the diet of rice and weeds resembling water lilies simply wasn't sufficient enough to nourish bodies ravaged by warfare, hardships, and stress. The diets of the prisoners were void of necessary nutrients and vitamins, and the heroic efforts of the doctors were often in vain.

Rice was fermented and yeast was added in an attempt to develop a medication for the most severe cases of malnutrition. The average amount given to patients was one-half cup of the mixture.

Dysentery patients' dietary treatment included powdered charcoal or rice which had been boiled to a thick, sticky, and gummy mass.

Some malaria patients were advised to lay in the sun, placing blankets over themselves whenever a chill developed. The hope was that these patients would be able to sweat away their malaria.

Topical ulcers were treated by washing the wound and then sunning the area. Those who had sulfa drugs covered the area with the powder.

There were hundreds of diphtheria casualties in the camp and there would have been many more if not for the serum that had been brought into the camp in November, 1942.

Our bathing facilities were makeshift. Some men created bath tubs using cans, buckets, or a piece of tin. For others, bathing under the eaves of barracks when it rained became common practice.

Flies were a serious menace and a health hazard. We dug trenches to be used as latrines. These trenches were about two feet wide, eight feet deep, and 40 feet long. We placed rails across the width of the trenches to keep the weaker men from falling in. These trenches would be filled with human waste within a matter of days. We'd then cover the trenches with dirt and dig new ones, trying to keep some semblance of order and sanitation in the camp.

The trenches were ideal breeding grounds for the flies and the tropical climate was conducive to flies and other insects. In an effort to reduce the fly count, the prisoners launched a campaign against them. Each prisoner was tasked with the goal of killing 20 flies per day. Later, we increased the number to 100 per day. The prisoners who killed the most flies in a day would be awarded a prize or a bounty.

Many men became fly trappers by placing fly traps over the latrines. Within just a short time, this procedure netted a milk can full of dead flies. Also, we discovered that putting flies over a steam drum would kill them.

We turned fly trapping into a game or contest. A game that provided a welcome distraction for the conditions we'd been subjected to and a game that, at the same time, made the camp a bit more livable. We measured and recorded the cans of dead flies. One prisoner gathered many five-gallon cans of them. Posters similar to Burma-Shave advertisements were placed throughout the camp, with slogans such as "Who's Going to Die—You or the Fly?"; "Brood Not on Beriberi, but Wipe Out Dysentery"; "If You're Broke and Crave a Smoke, Kill Flies"; "Caught Short, Can't Make It—Cover Up and Control Flies".

In July, 1942, 785 prisoners died at Cabanatuan. We buried our dead daily in trenches 10 feet long by six feet by three feet. Nude bodies were placed in mass graves and then covered with dirt. Sometimes there were so many bodies that they rose above ground level when stacked and all we could do was to heap dirt over them. There were times when the heavy rains washed the dirt away and the dead bodies were exposed. There were other times when wild dogs came and dug into some of the burial mounds.

After burying the dead, we always dug another mass grave for the next day's dead.

The high death rate continued until February, 1943. But even before then, Colonel Beecher, our American commander, announced on Christmas Eve of 1942 that for the first time since we'd arrived at the camp, we had gone 24 hours without a death in the camp.

The Farm

In August, 1943, the Japanese started feeding us a little better. A few carabao, a type of water buffalo, were brought in and butchered; we started a farm. Simple tools were brought in from the warehouses and farms in Luzon. Even then, we didn't have enough tools and many prisoners had to pull and carry grass by hand. Scrub trees and grass had to be cleared from the area to make the farm. Thousands of ant hills, some of them 20 feet in diameter and 10 feet tall, had to be leveled off. That was an unenviable task, as many of the prisoners who did that were riddled with ant bites, sometimes leading to infections and there were always snakes around the ant hills, looking to feast on the multitude of ants that resided there.

The Japanese supervised the making of the farm. Having farmed on a small scale in Japan, they insisted on building hundreds of trails and roads running parallel, and then other roads and trails intersecting at right angles about one yard apart. Yes, one yard apart. Prisoners were instructed to use wires to line the roads and to lay out the plots. Rows and roads were as tight as tightly-stretched string. Yes, it looked nice, but the numerous rows and roads were a great waste of labor and land.

A group of prisoners was escorted to the nearby city dump to dig up fertilizer for the farms. An accumulation of debris from ages past would be used to fertilize the soil of the farm. Carabao-driven carts were used to haul the fertilizer and soil that was retrieved from the dump. Twenty-four prisoners and two Japanese guards spent entire days digging and screening black soil that would be used on the farm.

Human waste taken from the latrines of the Japanese guards was also used to fertilize the soil. Because of the large number of Americans suffering from dysentery, excreta was not taken from the American camp. In moving the human waste from the latrines of the Japanese to the farm fields, the American prisoners used an oil drum which had been cut in half. The drum was filled with excreta, then suspended on the middle of a bamboo pole with a wire bail, and carried on the shoulders of two men. Forty men were assigned to this daily detail and since it involved considerable walking, those men were sometimes allowed to wear shoes. American officers were often assigned to this detail. Grass was also pulled and piled up to decay into fertilizer.

Work on the farm usually began at 7 a.m. and continued until noon, and then again from 1 p.m. until 3 p.m. Two 15-minute rest periods were given, one in the morning and another in the afternoon.

There was an attempt to grow a variety of crops, although not all were successful. We planted sweet potatoes, corn, radishes, mustard, okra, watermelon, pepper, onion, cabbage, papayas, squash, mongo beans, tomatoes, eggplant, peanuts, and rice. The hot climate, with a rainy and dry season, was obviously well-suited for…rice.

If planted at the right time, corn yielded some small ears. The radish and mustard yield was minimal, as insect pests ate most of the plants. We tried to make a homemade insecticide, boiling tobacco stems in an oil drum, but our concoction was ineffective. Neither was the one made by boiling soap in water.

Okra, eggplant, and tomatoes seem to grow well in the soil, but, unfortunately, we hadn't planted many of those items. Peanuts, watermelon, mongo beans, cabbage, and onions produced poor crops, partly due to the soil and partly due to the climate. Casaba and rice produced good yields.

A day of working on the farm was always a day to be dreaded. Every evening the Japanese would notify the American camp staff of how many farm workers would be required for the next day. The number varied daily.

The prisoners selected to work the farm would assemble near the farm gate at 6:30 a.m., where they were organized into groups under an American group leader. The Japanese were obsessed with counting and recounting the workers in these groups, always wanting to make sure that all men were accounted for before we started. I remember one time when the Japanese counted our group 18 times. We didn't mind, as being counted was much easier than working in the fields.

When the Japanese were comfortable with their counts, the guards would assemble, get orders from the officers and then relay these orders to the prisoner group leaders. After assignments had been disseminated, the gates to the farm were opened and we formed columns and marched to our assigned locations, where the Japanese again counted the number of prisoners in their groups.

Once inside the farm, the Japanese guards would take over the group. The prisoners knew well the reputation of the individual guards. They knew which guards were vicious and mean; they knew which guards were reasonable. So, during the process in which prisoners were assigned to guards, we knew what kind of day we'd have based on the guard we were assigned to work under.

We had given nicknames to all of the guards. Nicknames included Air Raid, Laughing Boy, Charlie Chaplin, Donald Duck, Angel Face, Mortimer Snerd, Doll Eyes, Saggy Pants, Old Dog Tray, Pop Muskrat, Big Speedo, Little Speedo, Major Mickey Mouse, Mabel Porky, Edna Mae Oliver, Dorothy Lamour, Farmer Jones, and Captain Moore.

A Japanese guard nicknamed Pop Muskrat had charge of the carpenter's detail at Cabanatuan. I was among that detail. The carpenters, all American prisoners, made and repaired tools such as rakes, hoes, shovels, mauls, litters, treadmills, buckets, boxes, threshers, plows, drags, and harrows. All of these implements were made by hand, using very crude tools, such as bolo knives, planes, augers, and saws.

A Japanese guard nicknamed Air Raid was one of the most detested guards on the farm. We knew that he always had some food items tucked away in the loft of a shed near the carpenter shop. When the Japanese officer had completed their morning inspection of the farm, Air Raid would take some rice to a secluded part of the farm, boil it, and have a mid-morning meal of sweet rice and bananas.

One morning, we had been working on an engine and had left a three-gallon bucket of gasoline in the shop while we took lunch. While we were in camp during the noon hour, the straw-covered roof of the same shop in which Air Raid kept his stash of hidden food started smoking.

The Japanese guards rushed to put out the fire, and, in their confusion, a guard nicknamed Many-Many Hammer

Head, picked up the bucket of gasoline and, thinking it was water, dumped it on the fire. The gasoline enhanced the fire immediately and the roof of the shed was immediately engulfed in flames. The Japanese opened the gates to the camp and the Americans came out and doused the fire.

At 7 a.m. the next day, 1800 prisoners were called to work on the farm. Guards arrived and lined up to receive their orders from the officers. They loaded their rifles and fixed their bayonets. Gates were opened and prisoners entered the farm in columns. After being counted and recounted by the paranoid and obsessive Japanese guards, the prisoners were sent to the various assignments on the farm. I was one of the eight carpenters who were last to be called that morning. We presumed that the fact that we were called last had something to do with the previous day's events, but we weren't sure what would happen next.

Instead of being dispatched to the carpenter shop as we were on most days, we were marched into an open patch and lined up for execution. A Japanese orderly ran to headquarters and brought back a Japanese officer's sword. The guard nicknamed Baggy Pants withdrew the two-handled sword from the scabbard and limbered his arms by swinging the sword over the eight of us carpenters.

One of the camp interpreters spoke to the line of prisoners: "There was a serious fire yesterday and considerable Japanese property was destroyed. We need to know which one of you set the building on fire."

None of my fellow carpenters and I spoke. Baggy Pants stepped forward with a raised sword and the interpreter continued: "Again, I will ask, who set the building on fire? There is no need for all of you to die."

It was then that a warrant officer of the Fourth Marines replied, "There were no Americans in the building when the fire started yesterday. We were in camp having our lunch."

The interpreter asked the warrant officer if he was sure. When the warrant officer replied "Yes" to the question, he was asked if he had seen any Japanese in the building. The Marine's reply was "No".

A chief boatswain's mate suggested that the hot sun was responsible for the fire. Baggy Pants did not agree.

It was then that I offered my theory to Baggy Pants. I pointed out that the loft of the building had held several large sacks of tightly-packed tobacco stems stored near the straw roofs of the building. I explained the dangers of spontaneous combustion and added that many tobacco farms in Kentucky, North Carolina, Tennessee, California, and Washington lost buildings every year to spontaneous combustion problems similar to the one we had seen the day before. Now, I knew that California and Washington were not known for tobacco production, but I knew that there was a much better chance that Baggy Pants would be familiar with California and Washington than he would be with Kentucky, North Carolina, or Tennessee.

As I outlined my theory to Baggy Pants, one of the other Japanese guards bent over to feel my knees. I figured out quickly that he wanted to see if my knees were shaking, and they certainly were.

Baggy Pants paced back and forth as he pondered the logic of my explanation. Nervously, we all waited to see what he would say or do next. We were very relieved when he eventually dismissed us and told us to get to work. We marched away quickly before he decided to change his mind.

That day at noon, my work detail mates and I had been discussing the "life or death" events of the morning, when one of my fellow prisoners suggested that he thought that Air Raid may have mistakenly started a fire by leaving a lit cigarette in the shed when he went to retrieve from his hidden stash of food. We'd thought about the possibility and hadn't yet ruled it out, when Air Raid came into the camp looking angry, frightened, and paranoid.

Upon seeing that we had survived the morning interrogation, Air Raid immediately called for the interpreter and then ordered the eight of us carpenters to line up again. We complied with his order. Consulting with the interpreter, Air Raid tried to force a confession from us, going so far as to slap one of my workmates across the temple with the broad side of a bolo knife.

The interpreter explained to Air Raid that we had blamed the fire on the hot sun and that Baggy Pants had determined that this was a reasonable explanation and had simply told the carpenters to get to work. Air Raid was relieved to know that he was off the hook and his demeanor changed with that news. Had it been determined that his lit cigarette was the cause of the fire, he would have surely received a thorough beating with a club, and would have likely then killed the carpenters for reporting him.

Although the idea of a farm at Cabanatuan made sense, it never worked in reality as well as it worked on paper. Very few of the American prisoners had farmed before. We didn't know much about raising crops. And farming in the tropics was much different than farming was in Iowa or Nebraska. Working in the fields in a tropical climate was dreadful, especially given the poor physical condition we were all in. And also, as we eventually learned, no matter how much food we produced on the farm, our diet remained the same. We lost interest in the farm, although we continued to be forced to work it.

More on Camp #1

During our lengthy stay at Camp #1, some of the guards were more tolerant of others and various means of punishment were meted out. A set of rules consisting of "Do Nots" was established:

- Do not whistle.
- Do not sing.
- Do not talk, except in the line of duty.
- Do not cross plots.
- Do not smile, except during rest periods.
- Do not sit.
- Do not stand idle.
- Do not sit on water cans during rest periods.
- Keep moving and keep alert.

Violating any of these rules almost always brought the wrath of the guards on prisoners. Prisoners who violated the rules of the camp were usually slapped, kicked, or hit with rifles, belts, or clubs. Some prisoners were forced to stand bareheaded in the hot sun all day. Prisoners were often forced to hit or slap each other; sometimes innocent men were drawn into these fights to make a pair or a foursome.

Prisoners were sometimes forced to kneel so it was easier for shorter guards to strike them in the face. Pick handles were placed in the bends of prisoners' legs and the legs then folded back on the handle, cutting off circulation.

Sometimes punishments were severe, even for seemingly minor rules violations. I remember one day when a fellow prisoner was caught stealing a bar of soap as he performed his daily work detail in the tool shed. That prisoner was severely beaten with a pick handle, then forced to stand at attention in the sun, holding the bar of soap for all to see, a poster boy for what could happen to any of us who violated camp rules.

As this man stood in the middle of the camp yard, each of the 30 Japanese guards walked past him. Each guard struck him across the back with their rifle, often striking the man hard enough to knock him to the ground. The man would then be kicked in the vital parts until he got off the ground. When the demonstration had ended, the man was carried to a resting place. His leg was broken, his arm was badly injured, some ribs had been cracked, and bruises covered his body— all for a measly bar of soap, which he didn't get to keep.

Another man was caught stealing peppers. Air Raid forced that man to eat three pods of peppers on the spot. A sign board was put up; it read, "Anyone caught pulling the vegetables will be severely punished." The man who got caught stealing the peppers was forced to stand at attention in the center of the camp, holding a pepper in each of his outstretched hands. At noon, he was given a beating by the guards and the sign was changed to read, "Anyone caught stealing the vegetables will be shot." Mabel, the Japanese guard who counted and kept record of the number of prisoners on the farm, gave the man 40 centavos (24 cents) and told him to buy some peppers. But after that episode, the prisoner never had much of an interest in peppers.

During the dry season, a small stream which flowed through the farm was dammed up in three places and hundreds of five-gallon cans were brought in. Some cylinder-shaped buckets were made and water was carried from the stream to the plants in the field. The sun was so hot that the water poured on the plants evaporated almost as quickly as it was poured. A 20,000-gallon water tank was built on the farm and a small pump installed to pump water into the tank. Irrigation ditches were dug in various directions; reservoirs were also dug, so water could be stored in various locations nearer to the plants. Canals were laboriously dug to divert another stream through the farm.

Japanese officers asked the American prisoners for suggestions on devices that could pump water without fuel. Some of the prisoners submitted drawings of things like windmills, treadmills, and hydraulic rams. The prize was awarded for the drawing of a windmill, but the Japanese opted instead to have us construct a treadmill.

The shafts and even the chain links of the treadmill were made Y-shaped from a piece of 2" x 6" x 10" board. A reservoir about 20' by 100' was dug on the highest point of the farm, where water would be stored. We were instructed to water the plants from 6 p.m. to 10 p.m. each day. This practice was discontinued when two of the prisoners escaped. From that time on, prisoners were forced to work barefoot on the farm, lessening the urge to escape.

Throughout the camp, numerous projects were being carried out simultaneously. For the prisoners, some of the work details were more desirable than others. Houses were picked up and carried by prisoners at times. One hundred men cut wood in the jungles daily; fuel that was used in the Japanese and American galleys. Hundreds of men were used to build roads in and around the complex. Permanent details were sent to various places in Luzon, Palawan, Mindanao, Formosa Manchukuo, and Japan. Some details, such as building bridges, roads, airports, docks, mining, and ship yards, were considered much more desirable than working the farms.

A detail of divers was returned to Corregidor to recover about seven million silver pesos (about 3-1/2 million dollars) from the bay. This money had been dumped before the fall of Corregidor in hopes of keeping it out of the hands of the Japanese. The divers recovered about one million pesos. (We later learned that the US recovered most of the rest of the money after the war ended.)

A detail of 300 men left Camp O'Donnell and went to Tayabas to build a bridge. Only 70 of that detail survived the grueling and perilous work. Those 70 survivors were later sent to join us at Cabanatuan.

Language difficulties and frustrations continued to be the cause for many misunderstandings between the American prisoners and the Japanese guards. Many prisoner beatings resulted from simple language misunderstandings.

Starting December, 1942, American officers were paid a small monthly amount ($5). Men who worked on the farm were also paid small amounts: Privates were paid 5 cents a day. Corporals and petty officers to warrant officers were paid 12 cents a day. A commissary was established and a few food items became available for purchase. That being said, the commissary could never meet the needs of the large group of prisoners.

The camp at Cabanatuan consisted of 100 buildings. Most of these buildings were made of nipa (palm trees) and covered with straw. They were about 24' wide by 70' long with a platform that ran through the center. Upper and lower bays or shelves floored with bamboo strips about 1-1/2" wide and ¾" apart comprised our area for sleeping. The barracks were light and cool, not bad for sleeping. But they provided an ideal place for bedbugs and the camp was infested with them.

Throughout our stay at the camp, death and disease were prevalent, so prevalent that the Japanese guards seldomly visited the camp. They wanted as little to do with it as possible, because of the conditions. After the guards had looted just about everything of value from the American prisoners, they resigned themselves to trading for any of the valuable items the prisoners might have remaining. Some of the prisoners had been able to hide watches, fountain pens, and sulfa drugs.

We had named many of the roads and alleys running through the camp. We named the main road Broadway. Other roads and alleys had names such as Halden Lane, Burro Alley, Santa Fe Trail, and Drizzle Drive. We called our headquarters Times Square. An open area of the camp was labeled the Polo Grounds. Homesick and stuck in a deplorable situation, we used these names as a reminder of happier days gone by and a home we weren't sure we'd ever get back to.

A path was made along the wire fence which surrounded the camp. American guards were assigned to patrol the inside of the fence to prevent escapes, while Japanese guards patrolled the outside perimeter.

Prisoners were divided into groups of 10 called "shooting squads". If someone from the squad escaped, the other nine remaining men were executed in retaliation. This punishment forced prisoners to consider seriously the consequences of escaping. Their escapes would result in the deaths of fellow soldiers. In the time I was in camp, 16 prisoners from Camp #1 were executed as a result of fellow prisoner escape; four prisoners from Camp #3 were executed for the same reasons.

By Memorial Day, 1943, 2644 prisoners from Camp #1 were buried at the cemetery. Casualties were high at other camps also, including Camp O'Donnell, where 1600 Americans had perished.

Two ships loaded with prisoners had been bombed or torpedoed, resulting in more casualties. According to survivors, one ship with 1800 prisoners had only four survivors; the other ship with 1600 prisoners had 450 survivors.

In an effort to thwart escapes and retaliate against them, the Japanese also threatened to reduce food rations and the availability of water for all prisoners. Realistically, it was a long distance between our camp and safety for an escaped prisoner, as the nearest US ally and safe place was 1800 miles away.

Some of the escaped prisoners sought refuge in various Filipino villages, but the Japanese retaliated against any Filipino village caught harboring escaped American prisoners. Inside the camp, we were all aware of the dangers and consequences of an escape. Life outside the wire fence seemed to be as tenuous as life inside the fence.

A Japanese guard company from our camp raided a neighboring barrio (village). How many Filipinos were killed and the reason for the raid, I don't know, but when the guards returned to camp in the afternoon, one of them had a bamboo pole across his shoulder with the head of a Filipino man dangling from it. The prisoners in camp rushed to the fence to watch as the guard walked down the road. As was required, we had to salute any Japanese guard as he passed. One of the prisoners commented in a voice that could only be heard by those standing around him, and not the guard with the head hanging from the pole, "We're not saluting you, you bloody S.O.B. We're saluting the dead Filipino."

Later that day, the head was hung from a light pole on the road by the camp. The Japanese wanted the prisoners to know the consequences of escape, for both the prisoners who might consider escaping and for any Filipino who would consider harboring an escapee. By the next afternoon, the head on the pole had begun to smell and attract flies. One of the Japanese sentries cut it down, placed it in a burlap sack, and gave it to the next Filipino who passed. An unwilling participant, the passing Filipino wasn't sure what to do. Finally, he simply bowed to the sentry, replaced his hat, and walked away, bag in hand.

On June 2, 1942, three young ensigns escaped from our camp. Months later in September, these men were captured on Southern Luzon. Upon being asked to identify themselves, they gave the names of three Naval officers who had been slain at Corregidor. They told the Japanese that they had fled Corregidor before the Americans had even surrendered to the Japanese. The Japanese were suspicious of the men and brought them back to our camp, where the men were forced to get on stage at an assembly and read a long speech about the impossibility of escape and the perils of the jungle. In the same statement, the men were forced to praise the wonderful opportunities and treatment at the camp. After reading their statement, the men were escorted to a Japanese military camp where we had heard treatment was extremely harsh.

Two colonels and a Navy lieutenant attempted to escape soon after the return of the three ensigns. Apparently, the Japanese "dog and pony" show with the three ensigns had not discouraged them from escaping. The colonels and the lieutenant were apprehended by American guards as they attempted to crawl out from an opening from a drainage ditch.

Upon hearing this commotion in the camp, the Japanese came into camp to investigate. They took the three officers into custody, beat them unmercifully about the legs and body, then took them to the guardhouse, where they bound them in uncomfortable positions and continued to beat them all night.

During the following day and night, the Japanese guards kicked and beat these men at every opportunity. Filipinos who passed by the camp were required to strike the three men.

On the morning of the third day after the failed escape, a Japanese burial squad marched past the group with spades. A rifle squad came and the men were unbound. The men had been beaten so badly that none of them was able to walk. One of the men was nude, except for his undershorts. A truck was stopped and all three prisoners were roughly tossed into the back of the truck. The truck then transported the men to an area near the corner of the camp. A short time later, we all heard a volley of gunshots. The Japanese guards soon returned without the three prisoners.

Occupants of the building in which these three officers had slept were also punished for harboring criminals. For 30 days, the occupants of this barracks were not allowed to leave the barracks and were given only small portions of rice to eat. This was apparently Japanese justice.

On other occasions, six prisoners were shot one day after going under a fence to buy food from the Filipinos. Two other men were shot near the hospital area and four other men were shot near the camp.

Prisoners to be executed were often subjected to horrible punishment before they were shot. It was difficult to understand the thinking of our captors, but we came to the conclusion that their reason for punishing prisoners of war as they did, was that the prisoners would then come to regard death as a relief from the punishment.

An instance occurred near the hospital one night. An American soldier was apparently trading some items with a Japanese guard. The American was inside the fence of the camp and the Japanese guard was outside the fence as they made their trade. When a Japanese officer appeared unexpectedly, the guard immediately blew his whistle, seized the American through the fence, and told the officer that the American had been attempting to escape. The remainder of the story is similar to the others. The American prisoner was severely beaten to the brink of death, then carted off and shot.

There was another instance in which a sick prisoner hid in a field. When the farm detail was brought in and counted, that prisoner was missing. A commotion followed among the Japanese guards and they quickly assembled and left for the fields to search for the missing prisoner. It wasn't long before we heard a song that sounded like an Indian war chant coming from the fields. Later that night, around midnight, a Filipino toted the prisoner to camp in a carabao cart. The body of the prisoner had been badly mutilated and beaten to a pulp. Numerous bones had been broken, bayonet wounds had been inflicted, and the corpse had been shot, probably mercifully shot. Prisoner group leaders were summoned the next morning and told to inform their men in the barracks about the incident and to warn them that similar consequences awaited any man who tried to escape.

On another day, a prisoner who had seemingly gone mad, crossed the fence at daylight. He left his wooden shoes at the place of crossing and disappeared into a sweet potato patch. A three-day manhunt followed. Manic guards searched the fields multiple times without success. On the third day, the guards abandoned the search and things returned back to normal in the camp. A week later, prisoners were removing some decayed grass from a woodpile when they uncovered the missing prisoner, still alive.

Apparently, the man had been getting water from the spigot near the guard shack, and had with him some raw papayas and sweet potatoes. In a weakened condition, he was unable to stand. He was carried to the Japanese headquarters and the American camp commander was summoned. The burial detail was sent to the cemetery to dig out a grave. When that was complete, the Japanese detail took the man to the gravesite. The story varies at this point. One version had the man already dead upon arrival at the grave. Another version had the man dying from a bullet to the head after he had been dumped alive into the grave. Either way, the burial detail covered the body the next day.

During the times when the death rate was high, dead men were placed in a shed which was used as a morgue. The burial detail would then place bodies on litters and transport them to the cemetery. One day, on the way to the cemetery, the men in the detail spotted some moving fingers from the pile of dead bodies. The fingers belonged to a man had been in a coma when he had been stacked with the dead bodies. He later recovered completely and eventually told the rest of us that his experience had been mortifying.

Survival

We entertained ourselves at the camp, often putting on shows that helped us forget about our circumstances, if just for a while. We had obtained some musical instruments; the Japanese had allowed us to have them. As a result, we produced some musical shows to entertain ourselves. At other times, other prisoners gave lectures concerning the jobs and professions they'd had prior to the military service. Many of these men had degrees from various US colleges and universities. Lecture topics included medicine, astronomy, history, horsemanship, agriculture, beekeeping, trials and tribulations of a private plane owner, insurance rackets, adventures of soldiers of fortune, cattle rustling, restaurants and unique places to eat, rescue of Floyd Collins, death of Colin Kelly, and many other interesting subjects.

Subjects pertaining to food were always among the most popular. The subject of sex was seldom discussed. No subject was off-limit, but whenever conversations got out of hand, the camp chaplains launched a clean-up campaign.

Church services were held every Sunday. At times the Japanese observed Fridays as worship days instead of Sundays. Services were always well-attended; many men participated.

In the camp, the Japanese showed four or five movies: The Marx Brothers in *"Animal Crackers"*, *"Pinnochio"*, *"The Ghost Returns"*, *"Japanese Bombing of Pearl Harbor"*, and *"Asia for Asiatics"*.

Thirteen hundred prisoners were transported to Bongabong to participate in the surrender scene of a movie that was said to have been called *"Down with the Stars & Stripes"*. Of all our days as prisoners, that day was the closest we had to an outing of any sort. A detail was sent to Corregidor, Bataan, and Manila to finish the movie.

Some of the Americans playing tank men in the movie created a near riot, as excited Filipinos that weren't aware a movie was being made thought the Americans had returned to save them from the Japanese. When they found out what was really happening, the Filipinos were, of course, disappointed. When requested to fill the Americans' canteens during the making of the movie, the Filipinos had obliged by filling the canteens with good old American whiskey from a secret pre-war stash. After their stint at movie-making, many of the American prisoners resolved to become movie actors if they ever made it back to the States.

Our camp had its share of distinguished men: Major Wing (the father of Toby Wing), Arthur A. (One-Man-Army of Bataan) Wermuth, Captain Robinson (Colin Kelly's co-pilot), Governor Rogers of Jolo, Sulu (Advisor to the Sultan of Sulu in the Philippines). There were also many other prominent men in camp.

Rumors constantly circulated through the camp. The collapse of Germany was a prominent rumor, one that went on for a long time. A rumor that we were to be exchanged for other prisoners also persisted. When the war ended, we asked the Japanese if they had ever tried to negotiate an exchange at any time during our imprisonment. We were told that they had indeed tried to negotiate an exchange, but obviously without success.

One officer told us that the Japanese had offered to release one American for every 10 American-trained technicians. The Japanese wanted the US to provide two-way transportation and also to surrender the fishing fleets at San Pedro, Pearl Harbor, and Vancouver to Japan. This officer told us that the US Secretary of State Cordell Hull had responded to the Japanese requests by saying, "No, we cannot meet this offer, but we will however give Japan a lesson in human decency or kill every damned one of them."

In the camp, the news we received was fairly accurate. All communication with the outside was forbidden, but our friends the Filipinos would smuggle notes into the camps.

Americans operated the power plants which supplied lights to the Japanese quarters and to the perimeter of the camp. (At that time, there were no lights in the camp itself.) The Japanese were deficient in some areas of technology and they often asked American technicians to repair their radios and communication devices.

A common trick employed by the Americans was to start a DC (direct current) generator and send a direct current through the radio and burn out some of the radio parts. Spare parts were kept in the power plants, and while the American technicians were repairing the radios, they used them to distribute and circulate news to the American prisoners.

Separating fact from fiction was always difficult with the news we received. The Japanese-controlled Manila newspaper was sometimes smuggled into camp. This paper presented a fairly reliable report...if reversed numbers of casualties were used. For example, if the article said that 15 Japanese and 450 Americans had died in a battle, we knew that the death count was probably the opposite of what the Japanese-controlled paper was telling us.

As death and transfer to Japan and other places reduced the number of prisoners, the size of the camp was reduced. Ingenious methods of disposal of the excreta finally reduced the files, and consequently, the dysentery rate decreased.

Around Christmas of 1942, some Red Cross supplies arrived at camp. The packages were part American, part English, and part Canadian. All packages contained food and tobacco. Each prisoner received 1-1/2 packages. The Red Cross food seemed to stop the beriberi temporarily. In addition to food, the packages contained other supplies that included clothing, cigarettes, and material to mend clothing and shoes. Also included were some toilet articles and athletic equipment.

The guards issued rations daily, carefully weighing and recording all food. Americans worked in the camp kitchen and even supervised them. There were some complaints about the men who cooked taking more than their fair share of food. The galleys (kitchens) of the camp were outfitted with shallow pots for cooking rice. Batteries or regular oil drums set in mud were used for boiling potato vines or other vegetables. The Americans cut wood from the jungles to burn in the galleys.

Dog meat was never served on the regular mess in the Philippines, but some prisoners trapped wild dogs and cooked them in five-gallon tins. Men would pool their rice and the dog meat would then be mixed with rice and made into a loaf that would be cooked over the coals. Removal of the head skin, liver, and intestines of the dog seemed to reduce the strong odor of the animal.

An animal resembling a fox, sometimes trapped in the jungle by the wood-cutting detail, was also eaten, despite its strong odor. Small frogs were also consumed.

The Japanese guards were fond of snakes. The prisoners often saw snakes when leveling off the ant hills of the farm. The snakes apparently ate ants from the ant hills. The Japanese guards would pay a bounty of four cigarettes to any American who captured a snake. The Japanese wanted the snakes captured alive; men who killed snakes were scolded and slapped.

One guard, who we nicknamed Snake Eater, would skin the snakes alive, run a stiff wire down the snake's throat and through the entire body, and then pass the snake back and forth through a pit fire until it was fully cooked. The meat would puff up when cooked and would become dry and white. Its taste resembled that of a pond perch. The snakes we caught resembled the species of a cobra, although we weren't sure what species they were. Either way, they were considered a delicacy by some of the Japanese.

As the war progressed, rations were reduced. By the end of 1943, rations were again scarce. Some American Red Cross food, medical supplies, athletic equipment, and clothing again made its way to camp. Also, 25,000 letters which had been censored in America and Tokyo were received. In spite of the previous censoring of these letters, the Japanese in camp insisted on censoring the letters again and two Japanese men were assigned the task of censoring. It was doubtful that these men could read English, as almost none of the guards in camp could speak or write English.

Distribution of the letters that came into camp was always delayed. Ten to 100 letters arrived at camp almost every day and anyone getting a letter containing anything of general interest posted the letter for all to read on the bulletin board we had concocted. Most of the letters, of course, did not contain general information and were of a more personal nature.

Transferred to Japan

On March, 1944, about 500 of the most able-bodied prisoners in camp were called out and told to strip to the waist. A Japanese inspecting party went through the ranks and selected 300 men for a detail to Japan. At that time, the selected men were given dysentery tests by the Japanese. All selected enlisted men were given a navy blue uniform from the locker club of Manila. Everyone was also given an extra pair of socks, shoes, and hat. Each selected man was also equipped with a canteen and a mess, and paid all of the money owed to him from working on the farm. The American officers were given a ridiculous-looking Japanese uniform. Warrant officers were not classified as officers.

I was one of the men selected for the detail to Japan. My fellow selectees and I weren't sure if that was a good thing or a bad thing, as we had no idea what lay ahead.

We were called soon after midnight on the day we left, given rice to eat and also some to take with us. The night before we had said our goodbyes to the prisoners who would be left behind, but everyone nevertheless assembled that morning to see us off. We waited for a prolonged period of time before three trucks showed up at 4 a.m. to transport us.

Herded on to trucks like cattle, we waved as we departed camp, leaving Cabanatuan behind in the dark.

Oh, the tragedies we had seen since we arrived in the camp many months earlier. We were glad to be leaving the deplorable conditions of the camp behind: the mud, the frequent rains, the sweltering heat, the bedbug infestations, the bamboo slats to sleep on, the farm and its miseries, the daily deaths, the almost unbearable stench. We'd take our chances with whatever lay ahead of us in Japan. At the same time, we wondered what would lay ahead for the friends we left behind.

Upon arrival at the train station, we were herded off the trucks and marched to the waiting freight train. After some cuffing, grunting, and shoving, we were loaded into boxcars which were already partially filled with a two-foot layer of firewood. The train departed at daylight.

Unlike previous trips, the guards allowed us to purchase foods from the Filipinos. Popped rice candy, dried rice cakes, peanuts, and bananas were available. The Filipinos, well aware of our plight, sometimes simply gave us food instead of selling it to us. As we prepared to leave the Filipinos, we also wondered about their plight, as they were now under the control of the Japanese. The Filipinos had been our allies and fought beside us as we tried to fend off Japanese troops. The Filipinos had remained kind to us even after the surrender to the Japanese.

The train reached Manila shortly after noon. Fifteen men were left at the station to load the wood and the baggage on to trucks. The rest of us were marched to Bilibid, where we were welcomed by some of the shipmates we hadn't seen since the capitulation at Corregidor almost two years before. We were immediately given commissary privileges and many men purchased small quantities of duck eggs, peanuts, salt, and bananas.

In preparation for our trip to Japan, we received some personal packages that had been sent from American friends and family. The Japanese had gone through the packages and confiscated most of the valuables and desirables. The package I received contained one size 6 right foot shoe. This shoe was much too small to fit me, but I was able to give it to another prisoner who had lost a right shoe at Corregidor. The package I received also contained some razor blades, handkerchiefs, underwear, towels, and some spoiled cheese, which I ate anyway. Packages for men who had died were given to men who had not received any packages of their own.

We were kept at Bilibid until April 24 of the following month. On that morning, we were called early and marched to the dock, where we were herded into the hold of a large freighter. The hold was very dusty, as it had been hauling cement, and it hadn't been swept before we inhabited it. The only ventilation in the hold came through the hatch. The hot and offensive air made the surroundings very uncomfortable.

As our freighter sailed past Corregidor and Mariveles, the mood in the hold was melancholy, as many of us came to the realization that we were no longer going to be rescued in the Philippines and any chance we had of escaping had now passed. When we were in Japan, there would be no chance of escape, as we would be in an enemy country.

Outside Manila Bay, submarine alert was sounded. All prisoners were ordered below, but the ship pulled through without mishap. We were in waters dotted with American submarines and where many ships had been sunk. Our ship was not marked as a ship that was carrying prisoners of war and was a probable target for American subs.

Food on the ship was extremely scarce and the small portions of rice we received were poorly cooked. Our cooking equipment consisted of a pot on the after deck and a cut-in-half barrel for a fire box. Fresh water was stringently rationed. A small portion of raw fish and a cherry pickled in salt was the usual noon meal. Seaweeds were added to the rice that was served at night. Nearly everyone who had brought a small portion of food from Manila ate that food early on in the trip to supplement the small rations.

The ship anchored at Takao, Formosa, where a 40-ship convoy was assembled for the remaining trip south. A freighter with thousands of Japanese troops tied up alongside our ship. We were surprised at the poor condition of the Japanese soldiers and the ship they were in. Junk cluttered the deck of the freighter carrying the Japanese soldiers; the soldiers themselves appeared to be inferior in quality to the Japanese soldiers we had previously encountered. And they all appeared poorly dressed.

More logs were taken aboard our ship while we were anchored; we then left port at sunset on the third day after arrival. We received a brief escort from a plane and a destroyer until it got dark and those escorts then left us to fend for ourselves against possible submarine attacks. The impending bad weather may have saved us from American subs, who again were probably unaware that our ship was carrying American prisoners.

We arrived and anchored at Shimonoseki, Japan. Upon arrival, a Japanese doctor came aboard the ship and did a quick inspection. He looked over the group of prisoners, felt a few pulses, then left the ship. We then sailed into the Inland Sea.

On Easter Sunday, April 9, 1944, we docked at Osaka, greeted by a few snowflakes. The temperatures were a far cry from the tropical temperatures of the Philippines. Some of my fellow prisoners hadn't seen snow before. By the time we arrived in Osaka, many of us had colds and were coughing constantly. Guards arrived to move us, but our ship was apparently late in arriving and they decided to keep us aboard overnight.

The ship became extremely cold overnight. A new set of guards with modern rifles came aboard. They visited the hold for just a short time, then quickly retired to the deck because of the offensive odor in the hold. Some of the guards distributed a few cigarettes to the prisoners.

Early the next morning at 4 a.m., we were called and given a small portion of rice to eat and an additional portion to take with us as we disembarked the *Taikoku Maru* after 17 days. We were glad to leave the miserable conditions of the ship behind. We later learned that the *Taikoku Maru* was sunk on May 17, 1944, by an American submarine. We had been fortunate that our journey aboard the ship had been a safe one.

Upon leaving the ship, we were marched to the street car line, where we boarded the street cars and were transported to the railroad. Some of the prisoners were surprised to see ice on the ground. The few stores remaining open were empty. There was very little traffic on the streets. The few people present stared at us. We saw a large sign with a picture of an American B-17 in crash mode, falling from the sky with wings coming off. We couldn't understand the Japanese writing that appeared on the sign, but we presumed that it was encouraging the Japanese people to join the all-out effort against the Americans.

Transported by street cars to a railroad underpass, we waited five hours for our train to arrive. Thankfully, we were allowed to sit on piles of gravel that had been dumped there.

The following day came and we were all still waiting for our train. There were many people loitering in the area, curious to see the lot of American prisoners. One Japanese man, who seemed to know all the American movie stars, told us that Secretary of the Navy Knox had died. When we asked him if he had any information on the war, he told us that he and his fellow Japanese citizens received very little war news. When we asked him if he knew our destination and fate, he said that he didn't know where we would be going. He also said that he thought we would receive better treatment and more food and mail now that we were in Japan. He speculated that the war would end soon, but later in the conversation, he also said he believed it could go on for a hundred years. Bottom line, he didn't know much more than we did.

Four Japanese girls were strolling near us. They were plump, rosy-cheeked, and clean, but shabbily dressed. Two of them seemed eager to talk, but the guards would not allow them to associate with the prisoners.

We were in poor physical condition and were neither dressed for nor accustomed to cold weather. Some of the American prisoners lay on the blocked streets, where it was slightly warmer because the sun shined down on them. When the remaining prisoners decided to do the same, a guard we'd quickly nicknamed Goering put an end to it and escorted us back into the gloomy shadows.

Late afternoon that day, a passenger train arrived to transport us from one epoch in history into another. We boarded the train, which didn't have enough seats for all of us. Some of us sat on our baggage, while others rotated sitting in the seats.

During the night, small wooden boxes containing barley, small pieces of oranges, squid, seaweed, and pickled radishes were distributed. Each prisoner received a pair of chopsticks with his box of food; some hot water with the slight taste of tea was given to us.

The guards were lenient enough to allow us to look out of the train windows, except when we were approaching a town, then we were required to lower the window shades. We didn't see any evidence of bombing. Despite the cold sleepless nights aboard the *Taikoku Maru*, we were not able to sleep on the train either. It was warmer, but far too crowded.

At 6 a.m., our train arrived at the Tokyo station. A Japanese doctor met the train and, with the assistance of the guards, confiscated all of the medicines which the American doctors had sent with us from Bilibid. Once again, we were left without medicine.

We disembarked the train and were hustled to more street cars for a 10-minute ride to another train station, where we would embark on a five-hour ride north.

As we looked out the windows of the train, we saw a few signs that Spring was approaching, including buds on the weeping willows. We saw winter crops, such as mustard. The guards in this train did not require us to lower window shades as we approached villages; we saw many barren, poverty-stricken villages on our route—villages that we presumed had been rendered more barren, more impoverished, and less populated by the ongoing war. As we passed some of the villages, startled women and children stared at the train loaded with white prisoners from a foreign land.

Moto Yama

At 1 p.m., our train stopped in a small village, where we disembarked. We were marched to a nearby park, halted, and given a barley ball to eat. The barley had been boiled and rolled into balls about the size of tennis balls. They were wrapped in a thin shaving of wood to hold them together. The ends of the wood shaving could not be bent and the barley had been exposed to dust and dirt, dirty hands, and flies.

When our "meal" was finished, we were again assembled for marching and told that we would proceed to the nearby mining town of Moto Yama (Mountain Top). The baggage and the men who were too sick to march were placed on a truck and hauled to Moto Yama. The remaining able prisoners embarked on an hour's hike to the same location. Upon arrival, we were halted and allowed to rest before ascending to our new home, which was about 500 feet uphill from a valley. The climb to the top of the mountain was almost vertical and we were exhausted by the time we completed our trek.

Our new encampment was enclosed in a wooden fence about 10 feet high. Immediately upon our arrival, the Japanese camp commander ordered us to assemble on a level between the barracks. A little man, the camp commander struck a Napoleonic pose, and yelled the word "Kiotsuke" again and again. We eventually figured out that he was asking us to stand at attention. Guards with bayonets rushed between the ranks of the prisoners, looking for men who were not at attention, without success.

With the help of an interpreter, the Japanese camp commander addressed us: "You are prisoners of war. You came over the Pacific Ocean to kill Japanese soldiers. You have fought against the Japanese Empire, a crime for which you cannot be forgiven. Now that you are here, you must work. You must work hard. If you do not work hard, you will be severely punished. You will be treated fairly, but not kindly."

The type of work was never mentioned. The interpreter was a kind-faced older Japanese man. Despite the loud and angry tone of the camp commander, the interpreter remained soft-spoken. He closed his speech by saying something we didn't think the camp commander had said: "Take care of your health so you will be able to work when you return home someday."

When the speech was over, we were instructed to go to our barracks and rest. Friends and shipmates got together in the barracks and were planning to live in the same groups, if possible. Navy and Marine men were together; Army personnel from the same units were together.

The barracks had a hall with no floors on the north side facing the valley. They were divided into four rooms with a half-inch partition between rooms. A pit was dug beneath the opening in the stall and the pit was cemented. The pit was designated as a "benjo", a toilet. The odor coming from the "benjo" was very offensive and ever-present.

The rooms had straw mats to be used for sleeping. These mats were about eight feet by three feet and were about four inches thick. There was no floor, but there was a board that was flush with the mat that ran around the square that enclosed the room. A brick fireplace occupied the center of the room, but it had no flue. Some 12" shelves, two feet apart, were used to store our baggage. Windows were sealed shut, with paper pasted over the seams. We had lights, but no chairs or benches to sit in. Each prisoner was issued three bowls: a large bowl, a medium bowl, and a tea bowl. These were the first food containers we'd been issued since our capture. Prior to that, we had to fend for ourselves.

At sunset, we were given our first meal at the camp. It consisted of a bowl of soup made from Irish potatoes and flavored with meat broth. Two Japanese women worked in the kitchen to prepare the meals, but after two days, they left, and Americans were assigned to the galleys.

Seven blankets were issued to each man, but, unlike Army blankets, the blankets we received were not woolen. Anyone who had brought a wool blanket into the camp had it confiscated. British and Australian overcoats were issued to all the prisoners. We already knew that cold temperatures in Japan were going to present conditions that we hadn't experienced in the Philippines. The good news about the colder climate was that it was not conducive to bug and insect infestations.

After we had been called out to clean the interior of the camp, each prisoner received a physical examination. Eyes, ears, lung capacity, and color blindness were checked. Many physical strength tests were administered, presumably to be used in determining what tasks the prisoners would be assigned. The Japanese doctors also administered some hypodermic injections. We weren't sure what these injections were for, but we complied nonetheless.

After the physical exams had been completed, we were all marched to the nearby town theater during a downpour of rain. We were all soaked upon arrival. At the theater, we were part of an orientation session. Many prominent Japanese officers were seated on stage and all of them were introduced. Some of those officers said a few words through an interpreter. One of the Japanese leaders, an instructor, showed us a chart which contained the layout of the mine in which many of us would apparently be working. He also showed us drawings of the various tools which would be used in the mine and gave us the Japanese names for those tools.

We had previously heard rumors that we would be leased to Japanese farmers or private families. There was a general feeling of disappointment when we found out that we would be working in mines instead. Mine work, on any level, was never known to be easy.

We learned at the orientation session that we would not be allowed to fraternize with civilians. Many of the Japanese in this area had not seen white men (or black men) before and they were amazed at the size of the Americans. Blond, red, or dark curly hair, and blue eyes attracted a lot of attention from Japanese civilians. Almost all Japanese were brown-eyed with straight, dark hair.

In the orientation session, we were instructed to work hard and to not stool in the mine. If we had to stool, we were instructed to tell our Japanese boss and he would tell us where we could relieve ourselves.

For tools, each man was issued a carbide light, a hoe with a pointed blade, and a pan with three sides and a bottom with handles on the sides for lifting when the pan was full of ore. For clothes, each prisoner was issued a miner's cap, a pair of tennis shoes, a pair of wrap leggings, and a pair of Japanese socks. Each prisoner was also issued two suits of Japanese work clothes, which were similar to uniforms. These uniforms were made of very poor quality cloth. The suits of Navy blues issued to us in the Philippines were confiscated and placed in storage.

On returning to camp from our orientation session, we were assigned to different barracks and rooms. Warrant officers were in charge of the rooms, which housed 16 to 18 men each. The men who were warrant officers received no additional compensation for their responsibilities. The room leader was expected to set an example as a leader and a hard worker.

Food was less plentiful here than it had been in the Philippines. Barley and a some kind of grain were issued instead of the rice that had been commonplace in the Philippines. Vegetables such as cabbage, potatoes, and beans were served occasionally, but in such limited quantities that we were always hungry. The staple diet seemed to be barley and radishes. The radishes there grew to be two to three feet long and three to four inches in diameter.

Every day, we received a spoonful of a substance which resembled peanut butter. This substance, which we called mizo, was made from bean meal and salt. It was our only source of salt. Lunches consisted of a ration of barley, a spoonful of mizo, and sometimes a slice of radish or a piece of ginger salt.

On the morning of our third day in the new camp, Japanese guards from the mine arrived and we were assigned to various details. I was in the "Jack-O-Soo-Caboo" group, workers on the 900' level. The guards marched us down the steep path to the valley below into a tunnel and one-half mile under the hill. The mine had been in operation for over 300 years. Ancient jig-jag steps led down 700' to the various levels, where work on the copper veins was in operation.

The first detail to which I was assigned involved a cable car ride down a 900' shaft and a walk through narrow, low, damp, dripping tunnels or corridors to the area assigned to me. The tunnels in the mine had been built for shorter Japanese men; taller American men had to bend over or stoop as we walked in the tunnels. The work was extremely exhausting and dangerous. Water dripped constantly and there was no ventilation. There were also no lights. We used our carbide lamps to see.

Some of the mine details consisted of loading small cars, approximately a cubic yard in dimension. We loaded the cars with rocks from a chute and then pushed it to another chute, where we dumped the waste rocks into a corridor that was being filled. At noon, work would be halted and we would eat lunch. The barley was usually sour and often caused intestinal disorders. While we ate, our carbide lights were refilled.

Work continued throughout the afternoons and we were usually allowed to quit working around 6 p.m. Long hours would be spent in the mine shifts. It seemed that the Japanese and the Koreans had priority and the American prisoners would be sent out of the mines only after the Japanese and Koreans had exited the mines and the elevator was available. Whenever Americans arrived on the ground level, we would march to a corridor and wait until all had arrived before marching uphill to the camp. The practice of carrying a load of wood uphill to burn in the galley was also started. Decayed mine timber and cross ties were brought from the mines and used as fuel.

A water-tight wooden box, 14 inches square and 3 inches deep, was installed at camp as a bathtub. All 300 men bathed in the same water, which was warmed by a small coal stove built into the side of the tub in a water-tight jacket. Obviously, bathing in water that so many other men had bathed in wasn't enviable, but we were so dirty from working in the mines that even a bath in dirty water was an improvement.

We'd been in camp for a few weeks, when an American major and some hospital corpsmen came into camp. They'd been at the POW camp in Shinagawa, Tokyo, and talked with some of the prisoners who had recently been captured. They relayed stories to us about the prisoners in that camp, including crews from submarines that had been captured and Flying Fortresses that had been shot down. The POW camp in Shinagawa was a man-made island constructed by prisoners of war. It housed "special prisoners" such as US Olympian Louis Zamperini, many Wake Island Marines, as well as the Commanders of the *USS Grenadier*, the *USS Houston*, and the *USS Tang*.

In our camp, conditions were in a miserable state. The weather was cold and the work was hard and long. Sanitary conditions were wretched and the meager supply of food was affecting the health of many of the prisoners. Beriberi was present; dysentery and hookworms were common; pneumonia, colds, and sinus infections were prevalent.

The new set of Japanese guards wasn't as quick to hit prisoners as they'd been in the Philippines, but there were instances of severe beatings.

At the end of the cold season in late May, the cherry trees began blooming and the dreary barren hills around us became more vibrant and cheerful to look at—that is, if we were above ground and seeing them during the daylight.

Cable cars suspended on wire cables spanned the mountain valleys like spider webs. The tailings (waste material from the mines) were sent to distant points from the mine to be dumped. We were told that the finely crushed rocks contained a chemical that would kill plants, and since the water from our streams was used for irrigation further down the mountain, the Japanese wanted to make sure the tailings didn't contaminate the water. The great pyramid-shaped piles of tailings and the continuous squeaking of cable cars that needed lubrication served as constant reminders of the dreaded mine and its confined quarters.

Every two weeks, we were given a day off from working in the mines. On this day, the toilets were cleaned and firewood was brought from the mines. Decayed timber and coal were burned in the galleys. As the weather turned warmer, flies and maggots made their appearance. Fleas were all over and they made sleeping difficult.

Each prisoner was issued a blank book and told to keep a record of his work and experiences in the mine. In issuing these books, the Japanese promised that if a man died, his diary would be sent home at the end of the war. Nevertheless, some men were afraid that the Japanese intended to collect the diaries, have them translated, and find out what the Americans' attitude toward the Japanese really was.

On "yasumi" (rest) days, besides cleaning toilets, transporting firewood from the mines, and cleaning drainage ditches, we were required to clean and repair equipment. Every prisoner who worked on this day was issued three cigarettes as a stipend. Also, toilet paper was issued by sheets after being carefully counted. Men usually carried the toilet paper in their pockets. Some men used the toilet paper to roll cigarettes when tobacco was available.

The strenuous labor in the mines and the lack of sufficient food eventually weakened even the strongest men in the camp. My legs became very swollen from beriberi and I became so weakened by an attack of dysentery that the Japanese removed me from mine detail and placed me on a detail for sick men. This duty was supposed be light work, however it consisted of lifting waste mud after the rocks had been crushed and the ore removed. Although this work was too strenuous for a sick man, I managed to last at it until August.

At 6 a.m. on July 2, 1944, we were lined up and assembled after a major blast had sounded from the mine. The vibration from the blast was so great that it had displaced some of the walls in our camp up to a foot in distance. We were told that the dynamite shed had exploded and that, as a result, some of the nearby houses had been flattened. Most of us remember that day clearly, as it was a day when we didn't have to work.

Ashio

On August 22, about seven weeks later, we were instructed to retrieve all tools from the mine. The following day, we were given our American shoes and our Navy blues, items which had been stored in a warehouse. We were paid all of the money which was owed us from the mine. Privates were paid 10 sen per day; petty officers received 15 sen per day; warrant officers were paid 25 sen per day. But the money was useless to us, as there was nothing for us to buy. Sick men and other men who worked in the camp instead of the mine, received no pay.

We were ordered to pack our clothing and prepare to leave the next day. We were split into three groups: 150 were sent to Ashio; 80 were sent to a dam site west of Tokyo; the remainder stayed at Moto Yama. Chinese, Dutch, and Americans from other prisoner camps were sent to replace the Americans who had been dispatched to the two other sites. At that time, there was a feeling that the Japanese were intentionally mixing nationalities in the camps to make it more difficult for the prisoners to organize a resistance effort or insurgence should the Allies attack Japan.

Our work details at Ashio were similar to those at Moto Yama, however somewhat more tolerable. At Ashio, we met Americans who had communicated with America. Some of them had eyewitness accounts of the attacks on Pearl Harbor; others had flown missions over Europe. Another was a pilot who had been shot down flying over the Solomon Islands. Some of the prisoners had been taken from the waters after their submarine sank. The Americans who had been captured recently were not as hardened as those who had been taken in the Philippines. Some of us had been isolated for so long that we were desperate and appreciative for any news we could get about America and the war effort.

We asked plenty of questions of those who had experienced the outside world more recently: "What were the new cars like?", "What were the new movies?", "Does the US have new ships, new planes, new weapons to fight the war?", "What's the talk about the war?", "How are things in the homeland?" And most importantly, "When do people in America think the war will end?"; "Will it ever end?"

From what I could tell, Ashio had about 300 prisoners from many different Allied countries. When we had arrived at Ashio, there were 13 American officers in camp. But all of those officers were transferred to a different camp three days after our arrival. The Japanese appointed a Dutch major who had been captured in Java to run our camp. His assistant was an Australian flight officer. About one-fourth of the prisoners in camp were Javanese Dutch, British merchantmen, or Americans captured at Guam. Many of the Americans in camp were members of the New Mexico National Guard and were of Mexican descent.

A Chinese seaman who spoke only a small amount of English was also a prisoner. He was skilled at translating the news from Japanese newspapers, which he was able to "borrow" before the Japanese officers read them. The Chinese prisoner would get a summary of the news accounts before returning the newspapers. Through his accounts, we were able to keep informed of the Japanese accounts of what was happening in the war. We realized that these Japanese accounts were most certainly different than the American accounts would have been.

With all the different nationalities, the camp at Ashio had an international flavor. Languages spoken in camp were English, Spanish, Dutch Javanese, Chinese, and Japanese.

In addition to the copper mine, there was a copper smelter at Ashio. Metals had been collected and sent to Ashio from many of the areas that Japan had subjugated. Items such as trinkets, works of art, household utensils, coins, temple bells, belt buckles, watches and clockworks, collar devices, and insignias were all melted. Prisoners who worked in the foundry occasionally managed to steal bells, bowls, and small jewel boxes before they were melted. Occasionally, the Japanese would do a camp search and confiscate these stolen items, but eventually the Japanese officers allowed us to keep the brass bowls to transport food to the barracks.

Late in September, the season started to turn and what had been comfortable temperatures turned chilly and cold. The grass covering the almost vertical mountain across the stream from the camp turned brown as the frost crept down the mountain.

The food at Ashio was both bad and scarce. Like Moto Yama, barley and radishes were common fare. Breakfast usually consisted of a small portion of greens and hot water. Salt was a rare item in Japan. Many prisoners would trade some of their possessions to obtain salt from Koreans from another camp who worked in the mines and who evidently had no problems getting salt.

Bartering was prohibited in the camps, but was often carried on secretly among prisoners. The Japanese intentionally kept salt out of the prisoners' diets, as they were aware of the fact that salt intake would cause the men to drink more water and more water would in turn cause edema or swelling of the limbs if taken in large quantities while on a low protein diet.

That November, the Japanese started sending some sickly horses to the butcher shop at Ashio. On butchering day, about twice a month, a cart from our camp would return from the butcher shop with a burlap sack full of horse bones, and sometimes with a keg of horse blood. The meatless bones would be boiled in a barrel and the broth which resulted would be issued to various sectors of the camp. Likewise, the horse bones would be distributed to different sectors.

The Japanese butcher was very good to the prisoners. He kept a battered, dented, and rusty wash basin with a small quantity of gravy made from horse blood on an open fire. He'd then send some of this gravy back with the cart pullers. In return, the Americans would give him a few puffs from a cigarette or an entire cigarette if we were fortunate enough to have any. (Tobacco in this camp was scarce.)

As autumn passed, the days grew shorter and the nights grew longer and colder. The work was divided into three shifts of eight hours each. One shift worked 8 a.m. to 4 p.m.; evening shift worked 4 p.m. to midnight; graveyard shift worked midnight to 8 a.m.

Sleeping conditions in the barracks were miserable. There was no heat and cold drafts swept across the damp ground. Illness increased and many men became paralyzed in their legs. Three men died due to illness and another man died in the mines.

Funerals at Ashio were gruesome. Dead bodies were placed in the brig. A Japanese carpenter constructed a coffin from half-inch pine boards. The body would then be placed into a coffin on a cart. Four men then transported the cart to the crematory, where wood was placed in the furnace and the coffin was shoved into the fire.

Two men returned to the crematory the next day with a clay urn. Under the direction of a Shinto priest, the men gathered some ashes from the furnace. Often, the bodies of the dead were not completely consumed and the remaining bones were tossed into the yard. When sufficient ashes had been gathered from the furnace, the men took them in an urn to a shrine and deposited them to await the end of the war.

Since the grain we were fed was so difficult to digest, the American prisoners had requested that bread be made from it. The Japanese sent some of the grain to a mill and had it ground into a pulp resembling a whole wheat flour. This was mixed with water, forming a sticky dough that was shaped into mounds the size of baseballs. The bottom of the loaf had a square opening to admit steam. The loaves would be placed in a square box with a lattice bottom. About six of these boxes were stacked over a barrel of boiling water, where the steam would pass through the lattice to the bread. The heat was confined with a flat board top. The layers of boxes would be rotated vertically until all had been next to the barrel. After about an hour of steaming, the loaf was done.

These loaves tasted more like dumplings than bread. There was neither salt nor leavening in it. It had the texture of liver, the color of chocolate, and was so heavy that it would sink instantly.

A loaf of this bread was considered a ration and, from that time on, our supper usually consisted of pun (bread) and some greens. Grasshopper powder (dried, ground grasshoppers) was also served. This powder resembled fertilizer, had a terrible odor, and an equally bad taste. We ate it nonetheless, because it seemed to be a good source for valuable protein.

Dried fish heads, fins, and other waste products from fish canneries were also served occasionally. A small amount of fish, usually in a bad state of preservation, was also served.

One time, about 40 boxes of shark heads and intestines were sent into camp. The shark stomachs were full of parrot fish in various stages of digestion and the bones and the contents of the parrot fish were also in various stages of digestion. When the intestines were boiled, the mass was very much like mud and had a smell similar to ammonia. No human stomach could retain this mash; on its way back up, the odor and taste were indeed terrible. On the other hand, the shark heads were edible and, as a result, were sparsely rationed. Some of the heads were boiled several times to prevent spoiling.

In November, about three tons of sweet potato vines were sent into our camp. Frost was killing all the non-frostproof plants, so the sweet potato vines offered another possible food source. All sick men and the men assigned to night duty were put to work sorting the vines, cutting them into pieces about three or four inches long, and then sacking them. The leaves were then stripped from the stems, rolled in toilet paper, and sometimes smoked. Every root that was found was eaten raw. Both roots and vines are sweet before cooking. Some of the vines, as hard as straw, were boiled in water and served. Most of the vines were stored while wet and, as a result, were covered in mildew. These vines were boiled and we ate them nonetheless.

Beriberi, scurvy, dysentery, and other conditions due to malnutrition were disabling so many men in the camp that only about 70 could be used for heavy labor at one time. Many men tried to get light duty. No one could be blamed for feigning illness. After all, we were being forced to sustain ourselves on food that no American would want to eat and we were forced to work for an enemy of the country we had intended to serve and protect.

Dysentery and beriberi finally weakened me so much that I could no longer perform the heavy labor. Eventually, I was assigned to light labor. This consisted of cleaning the barracks and grounds, cutting wood, working on the roads, mending shoes, and, with anywhere from three to 10 men, pulling the heavy two-wheeled carts. The cart detail hauled lumber, grain, coal, food, anything to be trucked. Motor trucks could not get into our camp, because of the narrow roads and the steep cobblestone hills.

Cart detail was a heavy and hard job. A lot of effort had to be exerted when climbing a hill with a load on the cart. The guard would sometimes ride in the cart, adding to the weight of the load. Straw ropes were attached to the cart for men to use in pulling the carts.

Despite the rigors of the cart detail, it also offered the advantage of being able to steal food, especially grain. We considered the act of stealing from the Japanese an honorable and acceptable thing to do anytime the opportunity presented itself. Stealing from our own, however, was disapproved by all; there were only a few prisoners who would do so. We dealt with the stealing among ourselves by having the largest man in the camp take a service belt, and, while the required number of men held the culprit, would give him a beating that would not be quickly forgotten. If the Japanese caught someone stealing from them, the Japanese guards would beat the man unmercifully and force him to stand at attention all day and night.

One day, we had transported several cartloads of Chinese cabbage into camp. A Javanese man was caught stealing one of the cabbages. As a result, he was forced to hold the cabbage with outstretched arms as he stood at attention all day in front of the guardhouse. The man was so hungry that he would chew and swallow three or four mouthfuls of cabbage any time the guards were not looking. We all thought it was funny that by sunset that day, the cabbage had dwindled to the size of an orange. Apparently, hunger has no law! We were surprised that the guards hadn't noticed, but with guard shift changes and lots of activity around the camp, the man who stole the cabbage at least got to eat most of it before he was dismissed.

With a lot of the foods we received in camp, the Japanese did a lackluster job of preserving the items. Several attempts were made to preserve the cabbage. Some of the cabbages were hung in nets to dry; some were cut and placed in barrels (without salt) in an effort to make kraut; some were buried upside down in the ground.

Had we received all of the foods that had been sent to camp by the Japanese army or the mining company, we would have fared much better. When apples, persimmons, or Japanese oranges were sent into camp, the Japanese guards were quick to pick through the items, taking whatever they wanted or needed. The guards would then delay distributing the remaining food items to the prisoners until a "yasumi" (rest) day was declared. By the time "yasumi" days were declared, much of the food had either been consumed by the guards or it had spoiled. Fruit that reached the prisoner was a rarity. Sometimes three prisoners would have to share a small apple that was rationed.

Shinagawa

By the end of November, 1944, so many men were unable to work that the Japanese army conducted an investigation and all disabled prisoners were then sent to the Shinagawa camp near Tokyo. Any man who was declared unfit was instructed to bring his gear and his belongings into the yard of the camp, where it was inspected. The guards confiscated almost all of the valuables. Some men had tried to retain some clothing by wearing multiple pairs of pants, underwear, or socks during the inspection, but the Japanese caught on to this ploy and the men were instructed to forfeit any extra sets of clothing they had.

We were called at 3 a.m. the day after the inspection. After breakfast, we were instructed to walk to the highway, where two buses were waiting. The men who couldn't walk were hauled in carts. The buses, which would take us to Tokyo, were overcrowded, but looking out the window of the bus, we relished the change of scenery from the dreary camp we'd grown accustomed to. Seeing the beautiful level land with winter crops was a treat.

As we drove through Tokyo, we noticed that none of the stores and shops had any merchandise in sight. People there seemed to be walking the streets with no apparent destination. We arrived at Shinagawa at sunset and were checked in by the Japanese guards at the gate. Once again, all of our possessions were checked and our names and numbers were recorded.

The Shinagawa camp was in an area that covered about two acres. It was encased by a pine board fence about 10 feet high with barbed wire at the top. The buildings were close together. One building housed the guards; one for the galley and store room; the other buildings for barracks with sleeping arrangements similar to what we'd experienced in the other work camps.

The bathing facilities at Shinagawa were the worst I encountered during my captivity in Japan. The bathtub was a wooden box with a tin bottom, about seven feet by four feet, and three feet deep. A fire was built under the tub to keep the water warm; we'd use wood, paper, coal, or anything that would burn for fuel.

Once again, about 300 men would bathe in the same water. The bathing procedure was to wet and soap our bodies and then rinse off…before we got into the tub. As more men with open sores, dysentery, tuberculosis, and other diseases bathed in the same water, the water became contaminated. There was a water trough in the bath house that was usually partially frozen over during the winter months of December, January, and February. Some of the men would break through the ice in the trough and pour the cold water over themselves to rinse off the foul-smelling water from the tab.

Prisoners from many different camps were sent to Shinagawa. The main hospital for Tokyo, which many of us called Hell Hospital, was housed on the premises. Shinagawa wasn't much of a work camp. The only labor the prisoners performed was camp maintenance—things such as cleaning the latrines, tending the gardens (every available foot of land was used to grow food), taking care of the Japanese guards' quarters, preparing their daily baths, and maintaining the muddy paths throughout the camp.

My first night at Shinagawa, after we had been searched by the guards, fed a supper of barley and a small piece of fish, and assigned to our barracks, a group of us got together to share our experiences in other camps and any news we had regarding the war. As many of the men had come from other camps, we found it informative to share our stories.

An American doctor joined us, asking us if we had any news about the war and relaying the news that he had. Apparently, American B-29s had been raiding Tokyo. We would see them soon, he told us.

Men who came from other camps introduced themselves and some of these men were reunited with shipmates or friends from the Philippines.

That first night, after supper, we were called to assemble. Quickly we learned that the Japanese guards at Shinagawa were going to be very strict, maintaining rigid discipline of the prisoners. At the muster (assembly), the prisoners were told to kneel on the ground and bow to the Japanese guards as they approached. Absolute quiet was required as an American sergeant would call out commands in Japanese. The assembly was more of a ceremony than it was an information or orientation session. We got the feeling that the Japanese merely want to let us know that they were in charge and that, during our stay, their wishes would be our commands.

About 10 p.m. that same night, after we'd retired to the barracks and many of the prisoners were sleeping, air raid sirens in Tokyo sounded. Immediately, all of the lights in camp were put out and we were called to march out of the barracks and herded to trenches which were about three feet wide by five feet deep. We were ordered to cover our heads with blankets and keep quiet, as the Japanese tried to hide the camp from overhead American bombers.

In the trenches, we could hear the faint hum of motors far to the south. Peeping from beneath the blanket, I could see light batteries probing the sky, looking for planes. Anti-aircraft guns fired intermittently, leaving flashes of light behind. Red fires could be seen in the distance to the south. One of the men in the trenches speculated that American B-29s had bombed a target. This was the first strike I'd seen by the Americans since the fall of Corregidor. When the air raid sirens finally went silent, we were ordered to return to our barracks. Many of us found it difficult to sleep that night; many of us who were new in camp hadn't experienced air raids before. We were happy to know that American forces were on the offensive against the Japanese.

Two days later, B-29s made a daylight raid. As before, we were marched out of the buildings and ordered to take cover in the trenches. But with a sky that was clear and blue, most of the men were able to get a good look at the B-29s. Many of us had heard about the B-29s, but we hadn't seen them in action before. One of the men in camp who had been a pilot that was shot down told us that the B-29s were flying at a height of about 35,000 feet. The planes left a long white vapor trail behind as they flew. Japanese anti-aircraft guns fired at the planes without effect.

Japanese Zero Fighter planes whined and zoomed as they tried to reach the thin-aired altitude at which the B-29s flew. Tiny, glittering, silvery crosses could be seen at the forward end of the vapor trails as the B-29s flew through the sky over Tokyo. Air raids became daily occurrences. Night raids became more frequent.

One cold January night, 300 planes raided Tokyo. Thousands of tons of incendiary bombs were dropped on the targets. Fires burned unchecked. Smoke and ashes filled the air. The practice of requiring the prisoners to vacate the buildings and relocate to the trenches was discontinued, as the air raids were just too frequent. During subsequent air raids, men were required to go to their barracks. Smoking during air raids was forbidden.

Shinagawa had a large quantity of medicine which had been sent by the American Red Cross, but the Japanese maintained custody of it. American doctors were required to requisition medications from the Japanese on an as-needed basis. Also, at times, the Japanese administered their own medications. Men in advanced stages of malnutrition were given a daily injection (in the thigh) of a liquid substance which resembled blood broth. The same needle would be used on multiple men without sterilization. One didn't have to be a doctor to understand the perils of such a practice. A spoonful of dried blood was also administered orally on a daily basis. Carbosome tablets were given to dysentery patients. Blood was drawn from a vein in the arm and injected into the thigh by a Japanese doctor.

Dysentery patients would receive a 10-day regimen of carbosome and report to a Japanese doctor. The patient would be instructed to remove his clothing and asked to lay on his back on a board while the doctor examined his lower intestines. The morning I was examined, the temperatures were below freezing and the room was unheated. The doctor injected me with a blast of cold air from an apparatus that resembled a bicycle pump. This was a painful procedure which produced immediate cramping. Some patients were restrained with arm and leg cuffs during the painful procedure.

I was told by men who worked on the hospital staff that bile had been taken from the gall bladder of a dead tubercular patient and injected into a living patient as an experiment. I was also told that a dead American patient's intestines had been removed and measured.

Dead prisoners at Shinagawa were removed from the camp by a Japanese undertaker and carted off in a wooden box on a trailer pulled by a bicycle. The dead bodies were taken to a crematory and then, days later, the ashes were returned in a box about the size of a shoe box. These boxes of ashes were then stored on a shelf in the barracks.

Barley bread baked in Tokyo was served at our camp in Shinagawa. The allotted portion of this bread consisted of one small loaf approximately the size of two buns. A typical meal was one loaf of bread and a bowl of thin radish broth. No grain was included, but small amounts of beans and fish were sometimes served. The Japanese were apparently of the opinion that sick men required little food and, as a result, portions were reduced accordingly.

Fourteen pneumonia patients were kept in one room. Having had experience in the hospital corps, I was assigned to help care for those patients. There were no beds for these patients, only straw mats. The only source of heating, despite the cold temperatures, was a charcoal bucket which was permitted for an hour in the evenings. An American electrician had concocted a small heating unit for water. We used a tea kettle to heat water for the sick men. The heated water from the kettle was placed in the men's canteens, so they could keep the canteens next to their bodies for warmth.

The only "bedpan" was made from half of a five-gallon can and placed into a wooden box slightly larger. Three or four patients would use this box before it was emptied. It was necessary to lift the seriously ill men to sit on the box.

Bed baths were rarely given. The unsanitary conditions in the hospital were difficult to imagine. Fortunately, most men were able to recover and were able to return home alive.

Another of my assignments at Shinagawa was that of a Japanese bath keeper. My daily duty was to heat the bath water for the guards. I cut wood to fire the furnace and filled the tub with water at 10 a.m. every morning. By 3 p.m., when some of the guards began arriving from their shift, the bath would be ready for them. This was considered an enviable job and had its advantages. When I heated water for the guards, I had all the water I needed for myself. As I was often working by myself with the guards on duty, I was able to cook any food I had managed to steal from the Japanese. Although cooking by the prisoners was prohibited, I was able to do so without being caught.

In January, a 26-year-old B-29 pilot from Oregon was brought into camp. He was in extremely poor physical condition and looked to be much older than his years. While flying from an airport in China, he had been shot down over Nagasaki. When shot down, the pilot's bombardier had been beaten and killed by the angry Japanese mob that had discovered the two of them. The pilot himself was stripped of his clothes and forced to wear a Japanese kimono as he was hauled through town hanging from a pole and beaten unmercifully.

After he was captured, he had been forced into solitary confinement and nearly starved to death. His only interpersonal contact was with Japanese military who had many questions for him, mostly regarding the B-29 plane he had been flying. As the B-29 was new to the American arsenal, the Japanese didn't know much about it and they were anxious to learn.

The weather in Shinagawa was cold from December until late March, when the temperatures finally began to warm and the trees began to bud. Even in March, we had occasional snow showers.

Air raids became more and more frequent. We heard stories that some Japanese cities had been reduced to rubble. Despite our predicament, these stories gave us hope. In February, 1945, numerous US fighter planes appeared overhead, seemingly taunting the Japanese. The Japanese Zero Fighters were no match for the US fighter planes.

In April, 1945, we were officially notified that President Franklin D. Roosevelt had died. With this news, the Japanese were interested to find out what impact FDR's death would have on the war. The Japanese forced the American officers in camp to write their opinions as to what would happen with American war efforts now that their leader was dead. The officers later told us that their opinions were unanimous—FDR's death would not alter the course of the war effort at all.

By the end of March, the boils on my head had healed and the swelling in my feet and hands had subsided. The dysentery I had was under control. We had received some supplies from the American Red Cross, including food, and, as a result, our diets had improved slightly.

Back to Ashio

On April 21, I was one of five prisoners designated to be sent back to Ashio. Early that morning, we were marched to Shinagawa Station, where we boarded a train. A great crowd of Japanese refugees was present in the station. Apparently, vast areas of suburban Tokyo had been burned out as a result of the American air raids and many Japanese had lost their homes. Japanese men, women, and children slept on the concrete floor of the train station that had been clean the last time we passed through, but was now cluttered with rubbish and reeked of urine and excreta.

Japanese citizens, sullen and aimless from losing their homes, moved slowly when the guards ordered them to move to make room for our transport. There were so many refugees in the station that we would not have been able to get through if the guards hadn't ordered people to make way.

We were crowded into a small area of the train, with the guards nearby to watch us. Hundreds of Japanese crowded on to the trains, many of them abandoning the bombings of Tokyo for refuge in the country or smaller towns. Most of the Japanese were calm, taking their misfortunes as part of their new lives. Some of them even ventured to smile at us.

The train could not accommodate all of the refugees who had been waiting at the station. Immediately after the train left the station, we could see the damage that the American air raids had inflicted on Tokyo. Vast areas which formerly housed factories, shops, and homes were now in ruins. Skeletons of metal marked previous locations for machine shops, assembly plants, garages, and hangars. Guards had instructed us not to look out the windows, embarrassed by all of the devastation that had been inflicted, but we were easily able to sneak peeks nonetheless.

The refugees were traveling with as many possessions as they could carry with them, including food. An aged Japanese woman near us opened a lunch box containing cooked barley balls with black beans. Seeing that we were obviously malnourished, she offered to share her food with us, but the guards refused to allow her kindness.

Upon arrival at Ashio, we were searched by the guards and then told to retire to the barracks. All of the men in the barracks were eager to hear of our experiences in the other camp and also the news we had regarding all the damage in Tokyo. One of the men in the barracks relayed the news that Allied Russian troops were currently assembling on the German border and were waiting for spring thaw before launching a major attack on Germany. Like Tokyo, Germany had been bombed thoroughly by Allied forces and fighting had intensified. The prisoner who gave us this news speculated that, if all went well for the Allies, the war in Europe would be concluded within a month.

After the Germans fell, the prisoner explained, the Allies would then turn their full attention to Japan. The prisoner expressed his belief that Japan would fall by early August. We were all encouraged by the news of the Russian offensive on

Germany and the man's optimism that, once Germany fell, Japan would not be far behind.

The following day, me and the other four prisoners who had re-arrived at Ashio were taken to the camp doctors, who would examine us and recommend us for a level of work detail. I had lost a lot of weight since my imprisonment and the doctor determined that I wasn't healthy enough to work in the mines. As a result, I was assigned to camp detail, which, in my instance, consisted mostly of pulling carts and sewing shoes. The shoes worn by Americans in the mines were similar to tennis shoes and were made of cheap cloth with rubber soles. They were easily torn and had to be sewn by hand.

Gardens in the camp were started. A Japanese gardener nicknamed Tumblebug was in charge of the gardening. Tumblebug was an excellent gardener and an industrious worker. Prisoners preferred gardening detail over working in the mines, despite the stench of the liquid excreta that they were charged with in fertilizing the plants. The guards at the mines were vicious. Tumblebug was a gentle man who loved gardening. He treated his plants with care, even placing little nets beneath the pumpkin vines to help the vines hold the pumpkins as they increased in size and dangled from the eaves of the building.

One day a disabled prisoner was working with Tumblebug and the two of them were carrying a keg of liquid excreta from the latrine. The tall American was in the front, carrying one end of the pole on his shoulder, while Tumblebug carried the other end of the pole on his shoulder. The keg of excreta was hanging from the middle of the pole. Tumblebug took a fall and the container of excreta slipped down the pole toward Tumblebug. It splashed all over him. Calmly, Tumblebug wiped the excreta from his face, walked over to a spigot to rinse off his clothes and body, lit his pipe, and calmly had a smoke before continuing his work. It was this calm demeanor that made prisoners want to work in his garden detail.

Soon after the gardens were started, the Japanese decided to start a farm about three to four miles from the camp. Whenever we had a day of rest from the mines, we were sent to work on the farm, initially clearing the ground and preparing it for planting. The farm was on a steep hill and, after we cleared the area for planting, it was easy for the rains to wash away the soil. The farm work nonetheless continued, as we replaced the soil that had slid down the hill and planted it with crops. Working on the farm in the pleasant temperatures of May provided a great relief from working in the cold, dank mines. When we worked on the farm, we took our lunch of barley with us and ate there. On a couple of occasions, we were permitted a rare recreational treat, the chance to go swimming in a clear mountain stream that flowed near the farm.

A hen was brought into camp and the Japanese sergeant announced that chickens were to be raised. The hen died on the fourth day after its arrival, from eating larva. The sergeant took one-third of the hen to eat and the remaining portion was fed to the 15 sick men who were down with beriberi.

Three goats were then brought into camp and the Japanese sergeant then announced that goats were to be raised. One of the young goats died almost immediately, and it was skinned, quartered, and boiled into soup. The goat was so young that there was barely enough meat to flavor the soup. The other goats didn't last long either, dying due to illness.

Two pigs were brought into camp next. Since food was so difficult to get, the pigs were fed weeds. Like the goats and hens before them, they quickly passed. Next came four white rabbits. Their delicate stomachs were unable to digest the coarse weeds they were fed. Two of them died from the weeds and the other two were killed by rats, all within a week. None of the dead animals ever went to waste. They were either consumed by guards or were used in soup and served to the prisoners.

About every third day, 10 prisoners were taken to the countryside to gather edible weeds (for human consumption). Gathering weeds in burlap sacks was a welcome relief from the dreary camp and the damp, dank mines. The countryside was beautiful. Flowers and plants bloomed. We appreciated the scenery and relished the fresh scents and fragrances.

Whenever a supply of medicine arrived from the Red Cross, the Japanese took whatever supplies they needed first, and then held the remainder for rationing carefully to the prisoners.

A Japanese interpreter nicknamed The Quack was also a doctor. He was present at all sick calls and would prescribe the treatment. Burning was an accepted therapy for all illnesses. I had beriberi. In treating my illness, The Quack put ink dots in the form of a cross on my stomach and also between and on the outside of my legs in a symmetrical pattern. Pieces of punk were placed on the dots and then lit on fire. This process, of course, blistered the areas. This was The Quack's treatment for beriberi. After the treatments, patients were left with rows of dots burned on their legs; others were burned on the hands, arms, or backs.

Sixteen guards were sent with us when we were returned to Ashio. These guards all spoke English and were courteous.

As had happened before, American prisoners were taken to Japanese camp headquarters and questioned daily. Among the questions I was asked were: "What is your name?",

"Where were you born?", "Are you married?", "How many children do you have?", "Is it true that Americans eat bread three times a day?", and "What do you think of the Japanese people?". The consensus among my fellow prisoners and I was that the Japanese were asking these questions, especially the question regarding our thoughts regarding the Japanese people, to determine how they would be treated by the Americans when the war ended.

Air raid alerts continued through the month of July, however the isolated town of Ashio was never bombed. Nevertheless, when air raids sounded in the coastal cities, they also sounded at Ashio. August brought even more air raid warnings. Prisoners were required to go inside whenever a three-blast warning was sounded. A flight of bombers flew over camp one night and another two flew over camp days later. We had heard that the American bombers were methodically eliminating targets and we figured that Ashio was on the list.

During a search of camp one day, the Japanese guards found a can of meat among a man's belongings. These cans had been part of a Red Cross shipment. The man who had been hoarding the can of meat was accused of stealing the food from the Japanese warehouse. He was given a thorough beating and subsequently forced to stand at attention in front of the guard house for nine hours straight for the following two weeks. Strangely enough, upon completion of his sentence, the prisoner was then given two weeks rest in the camp as a guest of the camp commander.

All of the Dutch and Javanese prisoners in our camp were transferred to a camp a few miles north of Ashio. This move resulted in better conditions for those of us left behind. The Americans cooperated better than the Dutch or Javanese had, and this left the Japanese guards with a better demeanor. Also, with the departure of the Dutch and Javanese prisoners, the food was prepared with more care and seemed to be more sanitary when prepared by the Americans.

A rumor spread around camp quickly that a large bomb had been dropped on a city in the south and many people had been killed. On August 15, 1945, all work in the camp was halted and the prisoners were marched in from the mines without explanation. A Japanese army truck was sent to the farm to bring prisoners back to camp. Even the heavy cart from the farm was hauled in the truck. The gates to the camp were all closed and all the Japanese guards seemed anxious. Some of the guards were crying. We weren't sure what was happening. One of the prisoners had unverified information that Washington and Tokyo were now discussing an end to the war.

When the American in charge of the galley requested that food be issued for him to use in preparing lunches for the mine the next day, he was told to wait. Darkness came and we still weren't sure what the reason was for the change in protocol. Roll call was held and, unusually, none of the Japanese guards slapped the prisoners. Unlike previous nights, when the lights of the camp had been turned off so night bombers could not identify the camp, the lights remained on.

The following morning, dawn came and again roll call was taken in an unusually polite manner. Still we received no information regarding the change in attitude and protocol from the Japanese guards. After breakfast, the American officer in charge designated a working party to go to the hill to collect firewood to be burned in the galley. I took advantage of the lull and repaired some of the wooden tubs, buckets, and stirring sticks that were used in the galley.

On the second day after the mine had closed and the camp protocol had changed, we were assembled and told that from that time on, we would no longer need to salute the Japanese soldiers. Only Japanese officers need to be saluted.

Just a few days later, we were told that we would no longer need to salute the Japanese officers either.

Soon after that, the American prisoner who had been accused of stealing the can of meat asked the Japanese officer who had disciplined him to return the can of meat. The prisoner felt empowered and pointed out that he had endured unjust punishment in being denied the meat which he had not stolen and indeed belonged to him. The Japanese officer was very apologetic when he told the prisoner that he no longer had the can of meat. Someone had broken into his office and taken the can of meat and a bottle of sake.

The Japanese officer asked the American what he could give him to replace the meat. The officer was sincere, it seemed. The American told the Japanese officer that he wanted to make a cake and he wanted ingredients for that cake. Flour, sugar, eggs, shortening, and milk. The following day, the Japanese officer returned with two cans of asparagus, a can of salmon, some barley flour, and some raw sugar. The day after that, the officer brought three eggs. And on the third day, he delivered a quart of milk. Finally, the American was able to make his cake. He baked it on coals, using toothpaste for frosting. We were curious as to where the Japanese officer had obtained the milk, as there were no cows anywhere close to camp. Another prisoner asked the officer where he got the milk. In pidgin English, the officer replied, "Woman".

With the end of the war obviously imminent, our American camp commander assembled the prisoners and told us how to model our behavior as we moved forward. He noted that we had received instructions from General MacArthur's headquarters that we were not to assault any Japanese guards or citizens upon our release. We were told that the War Crimes Commission would punish the guards accordingly once the war was officially over. He encouraged us not to take personal retribution against the Japanese, even though he acknowledged that most of us had reasons to do so. Finally, he instructed us to paint the roofs of our barracks with the letters POW (Prisoners of War) so American planes could identify the camp.

In the following days, fighter planes flew over our camp regularly. The first time one flew over, it dropped a Coronet magazine, a pack of cigarettes, a box of matches, and two packs of Lifesaver mints. From that time on, fighter planes flew over daily, dropping items into the camp: cases of cigarettes, chewing gum, clothing articles, and toilet paper. Every day was like Christmas for our group, which had been deprived for such a long time.

Church was held for the first time in camp on Sunday. There was no chaplain, but an Australian flight officer delivered a stirring sermon.

On August 30, we spotted a B-29 flying over. The plane circled, obviously making a practice run of some sort. When it flew over a second time, it dropped three or four tons of food into the camp. None of the parachutes attached to the food cartons opened and the food crashed into the mountainside. Some of the food cans were badly damaged, but we made sure that very little food was wasted.

Immediately, we gathered the food, hauled it into camp, and stored it. We were issued some of those items immediately—candy, cigarettes, chewing gum, and toilet articles. Food that required cooking was cooked immediately so it wouldn't spoil. That evening, we feasted on a very good stew, which contained many of the food items which had been dropped into camp, including peas, pears, corned beef, carrots, beans, peaches, sugar, and even lemon powder.

Among the items dropped were printed sheets that confirmed the news that the Japanese had surrendered. The form also stated, "The Allied governments will feed you. You will be evacuated as soon as possible. Don't eat too much. We will be back in three days."

Once the drop was made, malnutrition problems decreased rapidly among those in camp. Not to be entirely outdone by the Americans, the Japanese sent fish, vegetables, and barley into camp. They also issued an extra ration of toilet paper, a raw silk towel, Japanese drawers/briefs (a strip of cloth on a string that ties around the waist), tobacco, and cigarettes. Our feeling regarding the "late" Japanese generosity was that, now that they had surrendered to the Americans, they wanted to be remembered for treating the POWs fairly.

One day soon after, we summoned some of our favorite Japanese and Korean bosses from the mines, ordering them to come to the camp. Tumblebug was also summoned. At 8 a.m. the next day, the Koreans who had been invited appeared at the camp as requested and lined up in front of the Japanese headquarters. Understandably, the guards were nervous and apprehensive, not sure what would happen to them now that the Americans were the bosses.

The Japanese men joined the Koreans, as American men from various past work details motioned for their former bosses to follow them. They Japanese and the Koreans apprehensively obliged with looks of suspicion on their faces. The men were shocked when they saw what the former prisoners had in store for them. We had prepared a party for them.

We gave our guests many "party favors", including cigarettes, chewing gum, candy, coffee with sugar, food, and clothing. The Americans would call out to the Koreans, "Hey, Honcho". The Koreans would respond laughing. "Honcho rai", they would say, which meant, "Now I'm no boss. You're boss".

Tumblebug was such a favorite of so many of the men that he was showered with gifts. He received enough clothing to last him the rest of his life, provided he got home with all of it.

Leaving Camp; Home Again

On September 3, 1945, we were instructed to be prepared to leave camp at 6 a.m. the next day. Men were busy collecting keepsakes to take with them, exchanging addresses with friends, and making final preparations for departure. Lights in the camp and in the barracks remained on all night.

Reveille wasn't necessary the next morning. At 3 a.m., everyone in camp was up and around. Breakfast, including K-rations, rice with plenty of sugar in it, and orange juice was served. Men in the galley called continually for others to come and get a second serving of the sweet rice. Many men obliged.

After breakfast, all bowls, tubs, and buckets were left on the tables. There would be no clean-up duty that day. The Japanese guards were told to help themselves to the remaining food. Many of them began eating as much as they could, probably expecting many hungry days ahead of them.

At 5:30 a.m. that day, we assembled and we were asked if anyone wanted to remain behind in Japan. The reply was a resounding "No".

Before leaving camp, we took the guards' guns. We bade farewell to the guards that we had not asked to accompany us as guides to the railway station. (Some of the guards and the Japanese camp commander would accompany us as guides.) At the railroad station we boarded a train with men who had been prisoners at a neighboring camp. An American who had brought a large roll of parachute silk, decided it was too heavy to tote around. Seeing a rosy-cheeked Japanese girl in a shop, he opened the door to the shop and walked in to give it to her as a gift he thought she would appreciate. Not knowing what his intentions were, the poor Japanese woman became so frightened that she jumped out a low window in the back of the shop and fled.

One of the most scenic trips I ever took was the trip from Ashio to Yokohama. I'll never forget that trip. The morning sun was starting to shine in the mountain valleys as we reached the lowlands. Startled Japanese from picturesque farms and homes stared at us as we sped along the tracks. Almost every window on the homes contained a long decorative piece of colored silk hanging from it. Some of the Americans aboard the train had been so displeased with the treatment from the Japanese at the camp that they had refused to leave behind any clothing or discarded articles for our former captors to claim. Upon seeing some of the Japanese standing along the railroad, many of these same men showered the Japanese with items such as gum, candy, or used clothes.

Free once again, many of us were overwhelmed with emotions as we tried to reconcile the past and imagine the future. Our train stopped at all of the small stations along the way. There the Japanese provided us with hot water from which we made coffee or soup, using soluble coffee and sugar to make the coffee and bullion powder to make the soup.

We gave cigarettes or candies to the Japanese who were kind enough to supply us with hot water. Along the way, some men ate K-rations, a lightweight packaged ration of foods which had been used for sustenance throughout the war (by those of us who had not been captured).

We met some trains headed in the opposite direction that were filled with Japanese soldiers going home from the front lines. Many of them had large bundles of loot they had taken from China or wherever they had been stationed. These soldiers appeared sullen and resentful; none of them smiled or waved as we passed. One Japanese woman waved at us and then held up her hands as if she was surrendering.

Our train reached the suburban area of Tokyo around 11 a.m. That area was now a burned-out area with hundreds of hovel dwellings similar to chicken coops and made from scorched tin. Many miles of burned districts lay along the railroad. There was no doubt that Japan had paid a price for its treacherous attack of Pearl Harbor.

When we arrived at Tokyo's Shinagawa Station, we were politely guided to another train. We departed as soon as all of the men were aboard. An hour later, we were in Yokohama.

We found out later that the American Army had not yet entered Tokyo. Tanks, jeeps, and reconnaissance cars were at the edge of the city. The Army would enter the city a few days later. The city was mostly deserted; any people who had remained behind were hidden in cellars or garrets. Never before in the history of modern Japan had a conqueror set foot on their shores. Japan expected the conquerors to treat them as they had treated the countries they had overcome with their war machine.

When our train stopped at Yokohama, eight or 10 American Army nurses were lined up outside the train to welcome us. They dispensed sincere greetings and each man received a bar of candy as he disembarked from the train.

We boarded Army trucks and were driven to the medical center, where we were examined by the doctors and sprayed with DDT, a pesticide which would eliminate the fleas and lice that we were carrying. We were given some clothing and asked to fill out a form for a telegram that would be sent home on our behalf.

After the medical exams, we were sent aboard a Dutch hospital ship, where we would be fed and quartered. For supper, we received a meager bowl of soup and a piece of bread. However, there were no complaints, as we knew now that better days were ahead. We also received a meager breakfast until an American tanker provided additional supplies of food. American officers briefed us on current news before we were summoned on to the docks, where Army and Navy personnel were separated. The Army personnel were directed to board an Army hospital ship; the Navy personnel boarded the *USS Water* and taken to the *USS Ozark*, where we were given more clothing and a place to sleep.

Very early the next day at 3 a.m., we were called, fed, and placed on a train which took us to the Yokohama airport. Hundreds of Japanese planes were grounded in the airport. The reports we had heard about US air supremacy were evidenced by the sight of all those damaged planes.

At 9 a.m., three C-54 Skymaster planes were taxied to the air field. We climbed aboard for what would be a long flight to Guam. We flew around Tokyo, over Fujiyama, and over Yokohama Bay. After flying almost all day, we landed in Guam at sunset—four years to the day from when I had sailed westward from Guam to China. As we approached Guam, I heard an officer say that he had stopped at Guam four years ago. Sure enough, I recognized him as a doctor who had been a passenger on the transport *USS Henderson*. I spoke with the man and he told me that a friend, who had made the same trip in Guam on the way to China, had died in camp only three weeks before. We acknowledged our good fortune in survival.

B-29s lined the runways of the airport in Guam. Planes arrived and departed like seabirds, running various missions. At 9 a.m. the next day, we were again aloft in the air on our way to the Marshall Islands. That afternoon, we landed at Pearl Harbor, where we remained overnight until 7 p.m. of the next day. At 9:30 a.m. the following day, we could see California from our plane. Our arrival on US soil was a very quiet one. There was no yelling or kissing the ground. There were few people there to welcome us, except for a slew of newspaper reporters who wanted to know what it had been like to be Japanese POWs. Some men answered questions freely; others had no interest in reliving their experiences so quickly.

From the Oakland airport, we were transported to an Oakland hospital, where we were again examined. Red Cross personnel at the hospital asked us to send telegrams to our loved ones, telling them that we were now stateside, safely and happily on US soil once again.

I was flown to Memphis, Tennessee on September 13, 1945, where I was treated for various ailments, including ber-iberi, hookworm, and malnutrition. I was also given dental treatment and was sent home on a 90-day leave.

Home was Huntsville, Alabama, and I arrived there by train at 3 a.m. Given the hour of my arrival, I had opted to take a taxi home, not wanting to be too much of an incon-venience for friends and family who wanted to welcome me.

The full moon was sinking low in the western sky as the taxi rolled up into the driveway. I noted that lights went on in all of the houses in the neighborhood, even at that odd hour. There was no more sleep that night. Everyone gathered, anxious to hear about my experiences. Many questions were asked and answered that morning and in the following days.

Freedom

I spent three years and four months as a prisoner of war. When I was released from captivity, I held the rank of warrant officer. Prisoners received pay at the rate or rank held at the time they were captured. Prisoners were advanced at the rate or rank equivalent to the rate or rank of their non-captured contemporaries. Repatriated Naval prisoners of war were given their choice of duty by the Navy.

Since my experience as a prisoner of war, I relish living in this wonderful country of ours more than ever. I never complain about food. I never complain about taxes. I never complain about much of anything to do with our great country. I consider it a privilege to live in the US and the freedom it offers all of us.

As I write in this journal, it has now been three years and eight months since my release as a prisoner of war. Since that time, many unpleasant memories were quickly forgotten or blocked out. My health has improved significantly since my release and I've never again taken for granted the things I may have once taken for granted. I relish my meals, my comfortable bed, the simple comforts of home, and the freedom I have to do as I want.

My sincere hope is for no one else to ever have some of the experiences I had as a prisoner of war. As I wrote some of my recollections, no nostalgia remains for any portion of my time in captivity. I write these recollections in the hope that anyone reading them will be reminded how fortunate we are to live in a country that offers the freedoms that our country offers. And I sincerely hope we never forget those who sacrificed and died for the freedoms we're able to experience in our everyday lives.

Letters

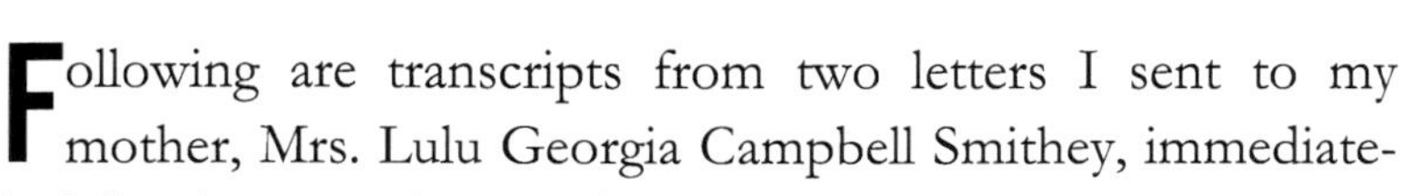

Following are transcripts from two letters I sent to my mother, Mrs. Lulu Georgia Campbell Smithey, immediately following my release and prior to my return:

Ashio, Japan

August 31, 1945

Our forces did such a wonderful job of reducing the Japanese cities that we can write the truth without fear of retaliation now. There has hardly been a day since the fall of Corregidor that pangs of hunger haven't been gnawing on us. Thanks to Uncle Sam, a Flying Fortress came over yesterday and dropped tons of food to us. Naval planes had already dropped some supplies. The Red Cross was unable to get any sizeable quantities of food to us prior to the armistice.

If you think we have been eating rice, you have overestimated the Japanese. We have subsisted almost entirely on barley and coreon.

We had a picnic at Cabantuan in the Philippine Islands compared with this place. I have gained 28 pounds. Everything is alright. Will be home soon. Regards to all.

Yokohama, Japan

September 5, 1945

The day we have so patiently waited for almost four years has come at last. It has been so long since I wrote an uncensored letter that I am confused.

We left our prison camp at Ashio yesterday at 7 a.m. Came to Yokohama via Tokyo. Our train has seven cars loaded with prisoners (about 475). This is one trip we won't forget. The contrast with it and the trip on the prison ship Taikoku Maru are too great to write about in a letter.

I might add that the Japanese cities are thoroughly demolished. A word picture couldn't convey the description of the ruins we saw. We were glad to see the Yank troops, equipment, and nurses. At present, we are aboard a Dutch hospital ship and are said to be going to a US ship today and sail for the Philippines and, from there, home. How soon and just what the plans are, I don't know.

I haven't had a letter from home since August, 1943; know nothing of what has happened since then. We never got any news of the war or happenings back home—except when a Korean or pro-America Japanese would tell us, or when a prisoner who had been captured recently would come in—which are very seldom.

The Japanese starved us and enforced very hard labor. I got down to 128 pounds, which was a heavyweight compared to some. Am back to normal weight now, plus some.

Must prepare to eat and leave ship. Will write again soon. Regards to all.

Talmadge A. Smithey
Military Service

October 5, 1931. Enlisted in Navy as Hospital Apprentice at US Naval Recruiting Station, Birmingham, Alabama.

October 6, 1931. Reported to US Naval Training Station, Hampton Roads, Virginia.

October 31, 1931-January 16, 1932. US Naval Hospital Corps School, Portsmouth, Virginia. Rated third from top in class of 100.

January 17, 1932-May 26, 1933. US Naval Hospital, Pensacola, Florida.

May 26, 1933-June 1, 1933. USS Chaumont, for transfer to Norfolk, Virginia.

June 1, 1933-April 20, 1938. USS Mississippi.

April 20, 1938-January 10, 1941. USS Oglala.

January 10, 1941-August 22, 1941. USS Dobbin, as ship's carpenter.

August 22, 1941-September 13, 1941. USS Henderson, for transfer to Asiatic Station.

September 13, 1941-April 9, 1942. USS Canopus, as ship's carpenter and division officer.

April 9, 1942-May 6, 1942. US Naval Battalion, 4th Regiment, 4th Battalion, "Q" Company, 4th US Marines' Beach Defense on Corregidor, Philippines. *USS Canopus* was scuttled on April 9, 1942, to avoid capture by Japanese. Officers and crew were ordered to Corregidor.

May 6, 1942. Captured by Japanese ground forces at the capitulation of Corregidor, the Island Fortress. Held as Japanese prisoner of war and various camps in the Philippines and on the main island of Honshu in Japan until September 4, 1945.

September 4, 1945. Liberated from the Ashio, Japan prisoner of war camp. Reported to the American forces at Yokohama, Japan and spent the night about the hospital ship *Tjalikga.*

September 5, 1945. Transferred to *USS Ozark.*

September 6, 1945-September 13, 1945. Enroute to Memphis, Tennessee, following release from prison camp.

September 13, 1945-March 20, 1946. US Naval Hospital, Memphis, Tennessee, for hospitalization (120 days), leave, rehabilitation, and disposition.

March 21, 1946-April 13, 1946. US Naval Damage and Fire Fighters School, Philadelphia, Pennsylvania.

April 13, 1946-April 29, 1946. Naval Officers' Ordinance School, Washington, D.C.

May 1, 1946-May 11, 1946. Radar School, St. Simon Island, Georgia.

May 22, 1946-August 2, 1948. *USS Portsmouth,* Philadelphia, Pennsylvania for duty as assistant first lieutenant and damage control officer. Also, later, first lieutenant.

September 8, 1948-June 15, 1949. University of South Carolina, Columbia, South Carolina. Enrolled as student.

July 11, 1949-May 27, 1950. General Line School, Newport Rhode Island.

June 5, 1950-May 13, 1954. Reported to Military Sea Transportation (MSTS) and served on the following ships:

USNS Private Elden H. Johnson, as executive officer military.

USNS General Alexander M. Patch, as executive officer military.

USNS General H.F. Hodges, as commanding officer military.

SS Washington, as commanding officer military.

USNS General R.M. Blatchford, as commanding officer military.

Sergeant Jonah E. Kelly, as commanding officer military.

May 26, 1954-June 25, 1954. Anti-Submarine Warfare School, Key West, Florida, as commanding officer, executive officer.

July 3, 1954-September 10, 1955. USS *Thomas E. Fraser* (destroyer), as executive officer.

October 25, 1955-December 5, 1956. Iceland Defense Forces at Keflavik.

January 24, 1957-July 12, 1957. Mine Warfare Staff Officer School, Yorktown, Virginia.

July 25, 1957-March 31, 1958. Mine Craft Headquarters, Charleston, South Carolina.

April 15, 1958-June 30, 1963. Inspector of Naval Material, Minneapolis, Minnesota.

Retired midnight, June 30, 1963.

Talmadge A. Smithey
Military Awards

Bronze Star Medal with Combat Valor. For gallantry in Infantry Action at Corregidor, Philippine Islands.

Army Distinguished Unit Citation with Oak Leaf Cluster. Awarded to officers and crew of *USS Canopus* for service with US Army at Bataan and Corregidor, Philippine Islands.

Navy Good Conduct Medal with Bronze Star. Awarded for first four years of good conduct service to enlisted personnel only.

Defense of America with Bronze Star.

Pacific Theatre of Operations with Bronze Star.

World War II Victory Medal.

Occupation of Europe and Asia. Served in Europe before the emergency was over in 1948.

Korean Service Medal. Transported United Nations' Troops to Korea.

Defense of Philippines with Bronze Star. Battle of Bataan and Corregidor, Philippine Islands.

Greek Expeditionary Forces Badge and Certificate (Greece). Transported Greek troops to Korea.

Ethiopian Expeditionary (Imperial Guard) Certificate, Unit Scarf, and Badge (Ethiopia). Transported Ethiopian troops to Korea.

United Nations Service Medal. Transported troops to Korea.

American Defense Service Medal with Fleet Clasp. For active duty in the Fleet.

Asiatic and Pacific Area Campaign Medal. For services in Asiatic and Pacific area.

European Service Ribbon.

Philippine Republic Presidential Unit Citation Badge.

More About Talmadge Smithey

If you enjoyed Talmadge Smithey's account of his experiences as a Japanese POW, you might also enjoy US Navy Supply Ensign Jack McClure's account of the Japanese siege of Corregidor in 1942. You can access this story, which includes a brief mention of Talmadge Smithey, on the internet at

www.historynet.com/besieged-on-the-rock-1942-siege-of-corregidor.htm

Also, you can read a bit more about Talmadge Smithey at the following internet links:

valor.militarytimes.com/hero/302012

www.mcmhc.us/?page=profile&hero=288

To the reader

Attached are photos of Talmadge Smithey and his family, including two articles about him that appeared in the *Huntsville Times*. Although these photos and the accompanying articles are not in mint condition, we thought you'd still enjoy seeing them.

A *Huntsville Times* newspaper article from August 8, 1963.

The Huntsville Times

SUNDAY, JUNE 23, 1985

CITY/State — Section C

Ex-POW Returns To Philippines 40 Years Later

By JULIE TAYLOR
Times Staff Writer

"Sleep, my sons, your duty done... For freedom's light has come. Sleep in the silent depths of the sea. Or in your bed of hallowed soil — until you hear at dawn the low clear reveille of God." — Monument at Corregidor

May 6, 1942: At 4:30 a.m., Talmadge Smithey was one of untrained sailors sent into battle at central Corregidor in the Philippine Islands. While emerging from the Malinta tunnel, they were hit with artillery fire until they managed to reach the battleline and drove the Japanese back 200 yards.

But by noon, the tiny island was surrendered because Major Francis Williams couldn't get reinforcements. The Japanese took captive Smithey and several thousand other young sailors and marched and transported them to prisoner of war camps.

Smithey barely escaped the "Bataan Death March" that took place a month earlier. After the battle, however, he survived one of the smaller infamous Japanese "death marches." Thousands of other young men didn't.

THAT WAS more than 40 years ago, but the retired U.S. Navy commander vividly remembers the details of the battle and his prisoner of war days as if they had happened yesterday. But more recently, he as well as the many other sailors who died during the war, have been honored by the Philippine government for their "heroism" during the battle.

Smithey, who lives at Three Forks in Northeast Madison County, was awarded a medal with the inscription "For the Defense of the Philippines." He was one of about a half-dozen American servicemen to be honored by the Philippine government for the first time since the war.

The Madison County native has also received other medals and letters of commendation — including one from President Harry Truman dated Dec. 14, 1945. The letter praises Smithey for the "great suffering" he endured as a prisoner of war.

As for his more recent award and tour of Philippines, Smithey said: "It was a good trip. It was condoned by the Philippine government. They are fine people and polite by nature — every one of them — and they did all they could to help us as prisoners even though the Japs tried to keep us apart."

He and the other tourists also helped dedicate several new monuments and memorials that recognize the sailors and prisoners of war who lost their lives in the Philippines. They also placed wreaths on the grave of 800 unknown soldiers who are buried together outside Santiago, an old Spanish prison in Manila.

ONE OF THE first steps on the tour was at Camp Cabanatuan — one of the former Japanese prison camps where Smithey was held captive for about two years. More than 3,000 Americans died at the camp and the battle of each once honored and forgotten in the wake of the monuments, Smithey remembered.

The five years of torture, starvation and disease at the prison camps don't show on 74-year-old former sailor's face. His features are striking: snow-white hair, sparkling light blue eyes, a pointed nose and a lean build.

He clearly remembers every day, and in some instances, every hour of his captivity.

"I try to remember the numerous times," he said. "Every day at camp was turmoil. The clouds of flies, mosquitos, lice, fleas, ants and them damn stinking Japs to put up with. Every day something horrible would happen. A prisoner would get killed or beat up or something. They would beat someone up as an example of what would happen to us. They wanted to intimidate us.

"We'd work for days building a road and a couple of days later tear it down or... and then move it. Every day something would happen to disgust you."

He also remembers having to watch some of his closest companions die at the hands of the Japanese. More than 500 prisoners died the first month Smithey was at Camp Cabanatuan. Almost 800 died the second month, he said.

"Most died from dysentery, beriberi, malaria and diphtheria," Smithey said. "There was no medicine, period. The Japs confiscated the medicine first thing.

"I had a lot of good friends and I saw a lot of them die... I hope that those that made it remember me for the tales I tell. If not it's good positive. They are liar from the truth I wouldn't describe about my experiences. I've lived through it every day, and all the time the experiences and times are with me."

SMITHEY WITH DECORATIONS

Was Business a 'Scam?'
2 Go to Court Locally Over Log-Home Sales

By RETA McKANNAN, Times Staff Writer

Two men face theft charges in Madison County Circuit Court this week stemming from an alleged scam operation that cost a local forensic scientist more than $18,000.

State Forensic Specialist Rodger Morrison contracted last year with Harrell "Hap" Boswell and Steve Baker to build a log cabin. The two, doing business as H&B Log Homes, advertised to construct energy-efficient, high-quality, log homes at factory-direct or discount prices.

In exchange for the buyers allowing people to watch the construction of the homes and go through the open house upon completion, the buyer would get the log home at an "at-cost" price. Morrison explained last week.

Boswell and Baker, charged with first-degree theft, are set to stand trial before Presiding Circuit Judge John David Snodgrass this week in connection with the case.

Morrison paid his money but never got his log home. "It was a scam operation, plain and simple," he said.

"Standard practice for building log homes is to make an up-front expenditure to have the logs cut because they are specially cut for a specific log home," he said. "Their objective was to stay just long enough to get prospects' money, so they'll swallow the bait," and then leave.

"They take the amount of money the investor has," Morrison said. "If you have plenty of money and will give them $8,000, they ask for $5,000. If you only have a little money to put down, they'll ask for $1,000 or $1,500.

"The contract shows that once the foundation is completed, a second payment is due, between $7,500 and $10,000 or $12,000."

Morrison said he became suspicious of the two men right away. They worked out of a local motel, he said, and had an answering service rather than a business phone.

"Then I found out they had no contractors' license."

According to Morrison, the men were supposed to build a foundation, and then get additional money for the roof and logs, but "it never gets to that phase. In an honest business, they are supposed to put in the foundation. I paid for my own."

In Lacey's Spring man had logs delivered to his lot, but they were not cut for the foundation that was poured. He said, "they were worthless."

Mo-
rison paid his money but never got his log home. "It was a scam operation, plain and simple."

A *Huntsville Times* 1985 article concerning Talmadge's return to the Philippines 40 years later.

Various photos of Talmadge in uniform and a photo of the
home he built.

Talmadge with niece Regina.

Talmadge in front of the old dam in Madison County,
Alabama.

Talmadge and brother Howard on the Flint River near
Huntsville, in a boat that Talmadge built.

Talmadge and Howard on the shores of the Flint River.

Talmadge (center) with niece Regina (left) and nephew
Howard (right).

Howard Roland Smithey, Jr. (left) and brother Scotty
Smithey, great nephews of Talmadge.

Tim Porter, friend of Scotty who coordinated the production of this book.

Made in the USA
Lexington, KY
06 December 2019